KILLER CONNECTIONS

Recognizing, Releasing, and Repairing Toxic Relationships

ZAKIYA MONIQUE

ISBN: 978-1-7335978-1-4

Dedications

I dedicate this book to LOVE! God is love, and without God, this book would not be possible.

To my first love, my father, Kenneth "Gator" Williams, who taught me silent lessons about relationships that I thoroughly understand today. Daddy, life hasn't been the same without you, but because your legacy resides in my hands, and your love rests in my heart, I choose to purposefully honor you.

Granny, Evelyn E. Williams, I miss you so very much, and truly, so much of me is you! Thank you for teaching me to stand for what I believe in, even if I stand alone. Thank you for displaying tenacity and leadership. We all miss you more than words can ever express.

Last, but not least, I dedicate this book to my "Kidd," Dorothy Mae Knighten. You sacrificed so much for me. You were truly the wind beneath my wings. You thought I could do anything, and sometimes, Grandma, I was so afraid. Yet knowing you had so much faith in me, it made me "run on" as you would say. You were the epitome of humility and service, and just to have even a portion of that makes me smile. Thank you for loving me. It wasn't in vain.

Table of Contents

Acknowledgments

Preface

Chapter 1 – You Betta Recognize

Chapter 2 – The Root

Chapter 3 – Warning Signs

Chapter 4 – Mind Ya Mind

Chapter 5 – Check Yaself

Chapter 6 – Stay or Walk Away

Chapter 7 – The Number of Completion

Acknowledgements

First, I'd like to thank my children, Raishaun and Robert, II for being so understanding when service calls. You two are the coolest, and I'm blessed to have you.

To my mothers, Idella and Shirley Jean. I appreciate the love and space you always give me to be me.

To my siblings, Teairrah and DeVante; sister/cousins, Trina, Kinyotta and Evelyn; The Knighten and Williams families; The Anna Cooper Family Circle; The Corbin, Pompey, Wilson, Martin, Crume, and Dickerson families; my business bestie, Precious, my Coach's Circle (Rhonda, RhanekaRhana, Nicole, Camy, Regina, Mishaun, Stephanie, and Anita), the ladies of Naomi's Nest, Dr. Beard, Dr. Paramore, Pastor Val Strong-Jarrells, and Jammie Cheek, who purchased this book 2.5 years before it was written and would not take their money back; and my village of love (Bobby, Ora, Nettie, Mary, Barbara Faye, Katrina and Helena).

I must acknowledge my beginnings, the City of River Rouge and Delray, because remembering where we have come from positions us to be blessed with the promise of what's to come.

PREFACE

My hand gripped the tree and stopped my fall, but my eyes saw nothing but gray. It seemed like everything happened in slow motion. As I closed my eyes, I felt a combination of rage, shock, and embarrassment fill my body. When I opened my eyes, I realized two things: 1) that my gray contact lens had slid out of place because 2) I had just experienced the very thing that my mother and grandmother had endured; the same thing that I said I would never allow. HE HIT ME… so hard that my contact lens slid out of place. He said that he would never hit me, but just that quick, I was a domestic violence victim, and I was only 18 years old. This was never supposed to happen, but that's the thing about toxic relationships—there is no control. There are no boundaries. If I would have known then what I know now, I would have left that day. Yet I believed things would get better. I was WRONG!

It's amazing how concerned we are about things like pollution and GMO foods, and rightfully so, but we don't take inventory of our relationships. Are you in a toxic relationship? Maybe you're not sure? So, to be clear, let's define toxic relationships.

KILLER CONNECTIONS

Toxic mean poisonous, harsh, malicious, harmful; something that causes death or serious debilitation or has lost its value.

A relationship is the way in which two people, places, or things communicate, connect, or act toward each other. A relationship is also sexual engagement between two or more people.

The combination of the two definitions above, give us an accurate depiction of what toxic relationships really are.

1) The way that we connect is no longer valuable.
2) The romantic/sexual connection between two or more is harsh, malicious, or harmful.
3) The way in which two or more people are connected can cause death or serious debilitation.

So again, I ask… are you in a toxic relationship?

This book will teach you how to recognize and release or repair toxic relationships. It is for you if:

1) *You aren't sure what a toxic relationship is.* As a teacher by trade, I have learned to never assume that anyone knows anything. So, if you aren't sure what a toxic relationship is, this book will provide you with a definition as well as root causes, warning signs, mindsets, traits, and real-life examples so that you can better identify, and in some cases, **prevent** being in a toxic relationship. After all, toxic relationships can cost you more than you can afford to pay.

2) *You are in an intimate relationship.* I know what you may be thinking, "No, we are good." I certainly hope that is the case, but wouldn't you want to know at the onset of a change that things were no longer "good," instead of waiting until you were in a full-fledged toxic relationship? Relationships have cycles and knowing how to recognize when things are going downhill in the worst way, may just save your life.

3) *You are currently in a toxic relationship, intimate or not.* This book is definitely for you if your relationship status on Facebook is "it's complicated" or if you find that you frequently have problems within relationships with your mate,

family, friends, co-workers, or church members. It's easy to point the finger at them, but we will do a self-evaluation too.

4) *You're not sure how to repair what is broken.* People change, and for as much as we would rather not deal with the hassle of mending the fences (or our hearts), there are times when we can't just release a person. Yet we don't want moving forward to feel like a life sentence. If this is your situation, this book is for you too!

This book, while written predominantly with an intimate relationship in mind, provides strategies for how to recognize and release or repair any toxic relationship, whether it is friendship or family. This is important because as we continue to evolve, our circles of companionship, friendship, and even those that we consider to be family will too. So, this book will help you make the necessary adjustments in your life, so that you can grow through your situations and move to the next level in life, love, and PURPOSE!

RECOGNIZING TOXIC RELATIONSHIPS

"You can close your eyes to the things you don't want to see, but you can't close your heart to the things you don't want to feel." ~ Johnny Depp

---

CHAPTER 1: YOU BETTA RECOGNIZE

The unfortunate thing about recognizing is that it is totally dependent upon senses. We recognize voices that we hear, aromas that we smell, food that we taste, people that we haven't seen in a while, and that tender touch of THE ONE! The only problem is that after we have been under the influence, be it seduction or physical intimacy, our senses are compromised. We no longer hear what is being said. Instead, we hear what we want our man to say. We no longer see him for who he is. We see potential and who we want him to be. We begin to think back to who we fell in love with, and quite often, that person is long gone. Yet we stick and stay because we are waiting for that person to return.

> *When we pulled up, I couldn't wait to get out of the car. I had made up my mind that it was over, especially after we were stuck in a traffic jam and he hit me again, this time busting my lip. I had known this man for almost two years and had never seen this side of him. I kept wondering who he really was and why he was acting this way because I really had not cheated or done anything that was offensive to our relationship. I still joke about the situation with the guy that he accused me of to this*

very day. I packed all his things, including the dirty laundry because I was done! When it was time for him to leave, he didn't want to go, and I don't have to tell you what happened next. "I'm sorry. I swear it will never happen again." My heart skipped a beat, and my stomach did flips. I was mad, but we had history. Plus, he had never had anyone who loved him like I did—seeking nothing in return, and I felt as if he deserved that. I know what you're thinking. What about what I deserved? I certainly didn't deserve a swollen lip or to be slapped because I had never laid with or touched another man, but I had been hurt as if I did. Come on now, nobody's perfect right? So, after talking for about an hour, we decided to work it out.

We were like newlyweds over the next couple of weeks, and then it happened, he stayed out all night. At first, I was worried. I couldn't sleep. Then when I heard MY car pull up, I was pissed off. So, I gave him the silent treatment. Now I understand that the silent treatment is not a consequence for poor behavior. Therefore, there were no real consequences for his actions. See, now I understand that disrespect must never be disregarded.

However, part of me wondered if I would see that crazy side of him again, so I just didn't say anything. Of course, it continued because what we allow always does, but I didn't understand why he started acting so crazy. I mean, it seems to me that if you were able to do what you wanted to do, you would be cool, right? Wrong! He would go through my cellular phone, curse my friends out, and hang up on them when they called, and if I wanted to go anywhere or do anything other than go to school, he either wanted to go with me or he had something to do and needed the car. I was no longer the sassy-talking, fun-loving Zakiya with a pep in her step; I was now sad and depressed, wearing dark, droopy clothes because I was... pregnant. This wasn't how my life was supposed to be. I had a plan, and it didn't involve children for another eleven years. I was so afraid, but he was so excited about his baby. Yet I didn't see him for nearly half of the pregnancy and then I found out why. I wasn't the only one expecting a child with him. Our relationship would never be the same or would our love stand the test?

Love, trust, communication, and time are areas that help us identify whether our relationships are healthy or toxic. Love is the foundation that holds the relationship together. Unfortunately, the emotional deficits of our past and/or becoming physically intimate too soon clouds our vision; thus, allowing us to mistake things like lust, obligation, or pity, for love. Then there is trust. Many people feel like trust is the glue that binds a relationship together. This is not true, but we will discuss that later. Trust is love's BFF because after the foundation has been established, we need to maintain a commitment and confidence in our partners. Communication helps us to maintain our connection or express disconnection as our love matures, and time helps us to build and heal as we remain in relationship. We have spent years debating over which one is most important, and if you asked the question on any form of social media or in a group setting today, you are guaranteed to witness a debate of some kind. So, let's talk a little more in depth about each of these.

Love

Love is the substance of things hoped for. Wait, no, that's faith. Love is <u>clearly</u> defined in the Bible and in most religious or spiritual settings. As we choose life partners, we can't HOPE for love to be present. We must be sure, and the only way to be sure is for that love to be tested. We never want that part, but tough situations or circumstances reveal the heart and character of a man. However, let me insert a very important disclaimer here. When I speak of tough situations or circumstances, I don't mean abuse such as how many women you will outlast or how many babies you will accept because of his cheating, or how long you will endure his beatings. If you choose to endure that type of pain, that is your choice. However, when I speak of tough situations or circumstances, I mean things like financial struggle, illness or loss of loved ones, for example.

Many of us don't make it through the test(s) because, as I said previously, we don't have true love. Some of us have pity for our mate because of his tough childhood, a disability, or the fact that he may have fallen on hard times. So, you feel guilty about leaving him because everyone else has. Yet that never works out because eventually, you'll becomes bitter and resentful about settling.

Prior to realizing that there was a title for what I was doing (relationship coach/strategist), there was a young lady who would speak to me about her relationship. After a few conversations, I couldn't understand why she remained in the toxic relationship. Keep in mind, at the time, my relationship was toxic too, but I didn't see it that way. I was loving someone who just needed to realize how good I was for him. Isn't it strange how we can't see our own situation? Anyway, she was beautiful, intelligent, and funny, and I was wondering why she would continue to be with someone who was so mean and disrespectful. God was showing me my own situation. So, one day, I did more than listen. I asked a series of questions, and BAM! I realized that she remained in the situation because of a promise she made to her mother-in-law to take care of her (the mother-in-law's) son. I didn't challenge that because it wasn't my place, but I immediately wondered why she made that promise when he wasn't taking care of her before his mother passed. I also wondered how someone could make such a loaded promise when people and relationships are subject to change. Well, after a whole decade of being cheated on and abused, she filed for divorce and broke the "promise" to her deceased mother-in-law. When asked why she stayed so long, "the promise" was one of the reasons.

Maybe that situation was a bit extreme, but if we're honest, sometimes we allow loyalty to get the best of us. Here is where we miss the mark when it comes to understanding a person's purpose in our lives. We quote the reasons, seasons, and lifetime scenarios, but somehow, everybody that we like, enjoy, or desire, ends up in the lifetime category, but that may not be God's plan. People remain in long-term and sometimes lifetime relationships just because a person was there for them during a tough time in their lives. While the display of reciprocity and loyalty is admirable, if you don't love that person, it will begin to feel like prison.

KILLER CONNECTIONS

We've talked about pity and obligation, so now let's get to the major force that is commonly mistaken for love—LUST! On my live broadcasts, I often say that we need to "close our legs and open our eyes" during the dating process because that is the time for interviewing. One of the principles that I learned as I was getting my degree in human resources is to "hire slow." This principle can also be applied to relationships. However, let me put a twist on things. Let's say that you are the human resources representative for a company where turnover is high, so your job is on the line. You must hire the proper candidate for a specific position. Would you get intoxicated during the interview process? I'm sure you quickly said no, correct? Well, you are the human resources representative for your love life, and some of us have high turnover rates (no judgment though, it's over and done), our hearts are on the line, we are looking for a specific person to love us, and we get intoxicated every time we have sex during this process. Didn't see that one coming, did you?

I'm not here to tell you that you should wait until marriage; that would be hypocritical because I didn't. However, if you are a Bible believer, then we are instructed to reserve sex for marriage, and now I understand why. I won't get into soul ties until Killer Connections Part II, but I will say that when you allow a man to enter your body, his location is not exclusive to your "pocketbook". He touches your soul, which is your mind, will, and emotions. After you have invited him in to share the experience, your judgment is impaired. So, when he lies, you say that he was only protecting you. When he hits you, you say that you shouldn't have provoked him. When he cheats, you say it's because you gained weight and don't do all that you used to do. Unfortunately, you're intoxicated, and no longer qualified to conduct the interview, but by then, you don't listen to the wisdom of those who are on the outside looking in.

To sum it up, God is love, and the Bible goes on to further define qualities of God as love. The Bible also refers to love as charity. Now, let's pause for a moment and give this some thought. When I think about charity, I'm thinking about giving to someone with a need, seeking nothing in return. For instance, when I give to the less fortunate, I do so freely and without need of acknowledgement or repayment. I believe this is how we are to give love, especially in relationships. See, it's easy for us to love someone when they are agreeing with us, but what about when they display an "unlovable" demeanor? Do we stop loving them? No! Now, I don't believe you should be abused, but love covers.

There is an old school song out by Teddy Pendergrass that talks about how good it feels when someone loves you back. The musical arrangement of that song just flows and feels good, but it is not realistic when he talks about a 50-50 love. Yes, it is amazing when we are loved in return, but it is truly unrealistic for us to expect that reciprocity will <u>always</u> be given and received at a perfect level. There are times when he may not love you back in the same manner that you love him, and vice versa. If you talk to a couple that has been married for years, they will tell you that there were times when one had to sacrifice more than the other, and there were times when one gave more effort than the other. We make the most of our relationships when we expect and prepare for these valleys.

Trust

Trust is another major area that helps us to evaluate whether our relationship is healthy or toxic. I believe without trust, there is no chance of a healthy relationship. However, I believe that without love, there is no REAL intimate relationship; it's simply an arrangement without a connection. I had a debate with a young lady on social media because she said that trust was the glue that held a relationship together. I disagreed. Why? Well, there was a couple that had been married for twenty-seven years. He was caught cheating. Her first instinct was to leave, but God instructed her to stay. The trust between them was obviously shattered, but guess what kept them together until the trust was restored? LOVE! See, if you truly love a person, your desire to be with them may cease, but your love for them won't. I believe that if you ever love someone, you will always love that person, even if you aren't in love with that person. So, trust can be broken, but true love can't.

For years, I've heard that trust was hard to build but easy to break. I think this is partially true. I agree that trust is easy to break, but I believe that trust is only hard to build when 1) we allow what people say to trump what they do and 2) we don't adjust our expectations based on what a person does or is at that time. See, having potential is great, but you can't make decisions or have expectation based on potential because it may never manifest. If we remain sober—no sex—and pay attention to actions instead of words, it will be much easier to decide whether we should trust a person or not.

One of the biggest struggles, however, is rebuilding trust after it has been broken. Some say that the relationship will never be the same. I believe the relationship can be better if 1) love is the foundation, 2) both parties are willing to recommit to the relationship, and 3) the opinions of others aren't welcome during the healing process. This means that 1) the offender must be willing to provide the necessary reassurance, 2) the offended must forgive and not throw the indiscretion up in the face of the offender, and 3) they both need to understand that rebuilding takes time.

KILLER CONNECTIONS

Communication

Thus far, we have discussed love, which is our relationship's foundation and trust, which displays our commitment to the relationship, and both are required for our next topic, communication. See, when it comes to communication, love will help you consider your mate's feelings when you speak. On the other hand, trust helps you believe what your mate says. Take it from me, communication without love can be brutal, and communication without trust is exhausting. This is where the need to check cell phones, wallets, car mileage, and credit cards begins—when you don't believe what he says. This causes nothing but stress, which ultimately has the power to shorten your life, so as I said before, it's exhausting! I used to be a private investigator, you will hear about that later, but my grandmother gave me a bit of freedom when she said, "What's done in the dark, will come to the light, and if you really want to know, ask God." So, I did just that, and He hasn't failed me yet. Warning, however, if you aren't ready to receive the answer, don't ask the question because sometimes what God reveals is not pretty.

Also, as it relates to communication, there should be a level of respect that defines boundaries for how we handle conflict. Yes, you should've a plan in place so that you are proactive when dealing with conflict because just as sure as you are two different people, raised in different homes with different ideologies, there will be conflict. However, without love and trust, our conflict turns into a fight, where we hit below the belt, saying things that we can't retract. Conflict is healthy, but fighting isn't. So, having love at the root and trust at the forefront helps us to maintain our connection or express the fact that we feel disconnected.

Communication also helps us manifest what we desire, and to destroy what we won't allow in our relationships. However, we must use the power of death and life that lies in our tongues for the right reason because murmuring, complaining, and talking about your spouse only brings what you don't want closer to you. We should, instead, speak what we seek until we see what we have said.

There are a few proven communication principles that I would like to share with you to help with the conflict in your relationship. First, I firmly believe that how you handle an issue the first time will determine if it is the worst time. If your mate stays out all night and there are no consequences, what do you think will happen again? If your mate disrespects you or crosses a previously-defined boundary and there are no consequences, what do you think will happen again? We are what we repeatedly do. So, if he is continuously doing the same disrespectful thing to you, that's who he is and what he does! Sure, no one is perfect, and wisdom leads us to choose our battles wisely, but disrespect should never be disregarded. Further, sweeping things under the rug only causes us to trip!

The second communication principle is that we should never walk away from a situation without the intent of coming back to address it. We must be open to the fact that not everyone has the same communication style. For instance, I can be very fun and humorous, and while I don't get angry often, when I do, it's not pretty at all. Thus, my communication style requires me to take a minute and discuss the issue when cooler heads prevail. Trying to force me to discuss the issue any sooner will probably lead to another issue. So, I take the time that I need to cool off with the full understanding that I will come back and deal with the matter later. There are some relationships where one mate likes to deal with things immediately, while the other mate likes to take a moment first. My suggestion is that you think about what is more important. Is it more important that you do things quickly or that you do them well? Whatever the case, don't allow issues to fester.

The third communication principle is that you must have a neutral-based source of resolution. When I worked for a law firm and dealt with the board of directors, there was always an odd number of board members so that the vote would never be tied. Well, in a relationship, there are two. This is where God comes in as the tie breaker for believers. His Word will bring resolution to those who seek it and peace to those who desire it. Then when you have the discussion, communication won't be one-sided or disrespectful no matter who is at fault. Each point of view will be respectfully expressed and then a consensus will be reached.

Overall, I want you to understand that ignoring issues, as I did when my mate didn't come home, only made matters worse. Then when I ended the silent treatment, we never discussed it. Instead, I just hoped that he would see how much I loved him, how good I was for him and decided to change. However, people change for two reasons, a sense of loss or a sense of gain, and based on his actions, he knew that he had me by the level of nonsense that I continued to excuse, so there was no sense of loss, and I had given him all of me, so there wasn't anything more to gain. I know that can be a tough truth to handle, but you grasp the fact that you can't change him, the less time you'll waste.

Time

Love leads to trust and respect. Trust and respect lead to effective communication, and effective communication leads to growth and maturity over time. Think about it, you love him, you trust him, you respect him, and you believe him. Now don't you want to invest more time in the relationship with him? Of course, we need to ensure that the feelings are mutual so that we aren't investing time aimlessly, but either way, you will want to be with him more and more when the other areas, love, trust, respect, and communication, are in order.

Time is the most precious commodity that we have. It can't be refunded or advanced. The world will lead us to believe that money is more important or that time is money. This is untrue. If I take your money, you have time to get more money; but when your time is up, money doesn't matter. Therefore, time is much more precious, as time is life. We don't own time. If we did, we would know how much time we have. We are simply managers of time. Therefore, it is up to us to spend our time wisely, not allowing anyone to waste it. Let's apply this to relationships.

Have you ever noticed that the women that are on the go, out and about, living their best lives, tend to have good men? Their relationships aren't perfect by far, but they don't have to spend every minute with him for him to be satisfied. Well, that's because in healthy relationships, time is not monopolized. Going out with friends and family is encouraged, and your man should be confident that it won't take the place of his quality time with you. He understands that there is enough love to go around, and he doesn't have to be with you every minute of the day to have a healthy relationship. In fact, it's healthy to miss one another sometimes. So, he wants you to take time to nurture your healthy relationships with friends and family. Then, when you spend time together, you consider on another when make plans and as a result, you both enjoy yourselves. Sure, there are times when you will surprise one another, but ultimately, the relationship is healthy when both parties have input in how quality time is spent.

On the other hand, when the relationship is toxic, there is a significant amount of time spent arguing, and eventually, isolation from your family and friends occurs. It doesn't happen suddenly, but slowly your relationships with those who love you, are eventually replaced with your relationship with him. He becomes all that you need. It's just you and Bae against the world, at least that's he'll have you thinking. If you suffer from low self-esteem or a lack of self-confidence, you may find the idea of Bae wanting you all to himself to be special. Then it goes overboard, and every time you want to go out, drama is the result. Meanwhile, your family and friends miss you because the truth is, they aren't against you.

So, there must be a mutual respect when it comes to time, as both parties had a life prior to entering the relationship. If time spent with others doesn't conflict with the boundaries that you have mutually established as a couple, then you should be able to have friends and activities that don't always involve your mate. Also, your mate should respect your time, honor his word, and not leave you waiting. Again, time is the most precious commodity that we have. We don't own it; we simply manage it. Therefore, we shouldn't allow anyone to waste it! Wasting time is really wasting life.

CHAPTER 2: THE ROOT

In order to get through something, I believe that we need to understand it to a certain degree. Over the years, I've learned to deal with ROOT ISSUES because if we keep picking the rotten fruit from the tree, but never address the tree's roots, the rotten fruit continues to grow. What do I mean? Well, until we understand why we do what we do, why we allow what we allow, or why we hold on to who has already left, we will never truly prepare for God's best. So, before we go any further, I want to discuss some root causes of toxic relationships because understanding the root issues can possibly keep us from entering these types of relationships again.

Poor Examples of Relationships

Unfortunately, many of us live in fear of repeating the very things that we endured or witnessed growing up. Now, before you disagree, remember that the statement is not all inclusive because I know many people who grew up one way, but when they were exposed to something better, they chose a different route. However, take a moment to think of your life. Did you witness a toxic relationship growing up? If so, did you make some decisions about what you would accept because of what you saw? Did you want a man like your father? Did you want to be like your mother? See, I never saw a man fight my mother, but I surely saw her bruised and beaten. I knew that I didn't want that for myself, and I was so focused on <u>not</u> allowing what happened to my mother to happen to me, that as I stood by that tree, I realized that I drew it closer by operating in fear. Fear brings the very thing that we don't want closer to us, so the answer here is to not be so fearfully and intently focused on what you don't want, but instead, make decisions and sacrifices for what you DO want.

When we are dating, we should find out what type of baggage the person has. Understand this, we all have baggage, but there is someone with the patience and wisdom to help you unpack and restore. There is indeed a lid for every pot. We need to know what a person has been exposed to because truly, we are dating their childhood too. Therefore, it's called dating and not mating because our eyes should be open, and our legs should be shut, but that will be further discussed in Killer Connections Part II.

Now I have a question for you. If your mate has never been exposed to healthy relationships or a healthy environment, can we truly expect him to create this type of environment or relationship? Or do you believe that everyone has been exposed to some type of healthy relationship or environment? See, I believe that we are all exposed to some type of healthy relationship, even if they are fictitious. Think about it. We all have or had an image of how our wedding day and marriage will be, but where did we get these views? Some of us watched our parents, grandparents, and other family members while the rest of us depended on external relationships, even those on television. We watched James and Florida Evans struggle but remain in love and integrity. We watched George and Louise Jefferson move on up but remain true to who they were. We watched Cliff and Claire Huxtable teach their children life lessons and how to earn their own education and money, even though they were affluent. So, by the time we got to our relationships, we already had an idea of how roles would be assumed, and tasks would be divided. Sometimes, this works, but often times, it doesn't; especially when these assumptions are never communicated or shared. Here is an example:

A couple cohabitated for seven years. They had two children. Both worked, lived in a nice home, and decided to get married. After they married, the husband asked the wife when she planned on submitting her work resignation. She was confused. She told him that she planned to continue to work and asked why he thought she would quit. He told her that as husband and wife, things should be more traditional with him being the breadwinner and her being the stay-at-home mom. She disagreed and this caused a great strain on their marriage, as he believed that she wasn't allowing him to "be the man" and take care of her in the same way that his father had taken care of his mother. This led to a separation.

All in all, we can't leave anything to question, especially when it comes to marriage. We can never assume that our mate shares our views about roles, responsibilities, or anything for that matter. We must communicate because we all come with preconceived notions about how things should be, and if these notions aren't accepted by our mate, then it impacts our ability to RELATE to one another.

Abandonment/Trust Issues

Abandonment issues will cause you to remain in a place longer than you should be there. It will also cause you to hold on so tight to something that you either ruin it or lose it. This reminds me of my favorite pair of shorts.

It was the summer of 1994, and every day, I was hanging with my friends. I had a pair of white shorts that fit just right in all the right places, don't judge me. I loved those shorts. Well, one day, all of that hanging out and fast food eating caught up with me, and when I tried to slide them on, it was an all-out war that I lost! Guess what? They were still in good shape, but because I had never had shorts that fit that way, I held on to those shorts until they were no good instead of releasing them to someone who could fit them when I couldn't.

This is what we do in relationships. We have never had someone so fine, driven, or thoughtful, and we squeeze tighter and tighter because of our own insecurities. We want him to stay forever. As a result, either he will break loose and never return because you smothered him, or he will realize the power that he has over you because you are so afraid for him to leave. This is how many women are manipulated. See, when the wrong guy knows that you are afraid to lose him, it's OVER! You will be viewed as a doormat. He will continue to push the bar to see what all you will accept. In fact, some guys believe that your love for them is displayed by how much foolishness you take. So, if you are afraid to lose him and he knows that, prepare to go through the ringer a few times, unless he is a REAL MAN. I often tell my daughter, anyone that you are too afraid to walk away from already has too much power over you.

There is another aspect of abandonment that we need to explore. It makes me think of the Oedipus Electra Complex, meaning how a girl connects with her father and how a boy connects with his mother is KEY! Think about it. When a young man is deprived of that special bond with his mother or it is tainted by her putting a man or an addiction first, for example, he is wounded and functioning with an emotional disability. I know what you are thinking… *my man was raised by his grandmother, stepmother, or aunt.* Nope, it's not the same thing. See, I was raised by my grandmother and aunt, and for many years, I struggled with emotional bonding because I felt that if a parent can betray you, anyone can. I was emotionally unavailable and numb. I've since been healed, but I still understand the struggle all too well. When a guy has been abandoned or mistreated by his "first love," his subsequent relationships tend to suffer until he is healed.

Then there are trust issues. There is nothing worse than making your current mate pay for mistakes that occurred in past relationships. However, we do it all the time for a couple of reasons. The first and most common reason is that we don't allow ourselves time to heal between relationships. I know you have heard the old saying, "The best way to get over one is to get another one." So, you run out and meet another guy, and after a while, you realize that this new person has some of your ex's characteristics. Then you start to have the same problems in the new relationship that you had in the past relationship. Why? Well, you carried the same toxic ingredients into the new relationship that existed in the past relationship, so expecting anything different is insanity.

Our trust issues are also fueled by our own expectations. See, ever since I had my first boyfriend at twelve years old, whenever I met a new guy, my main expectation was for him to be "better" than my ex. I know what you are thinking, twelve? Yes, twelve! I went all the way back to the root of the behavior. Here's what led to the complex that I developed.

It was June, and for as much as I loved school, I was kind of happy to be out. The pressure of being *the* honor student was heavy at times, and I just wanted a break. Besides, I had a boyfriend, and talking to him on the roof all night—our apartments were connected—was hard when it was time to function at optimal level the next day at school. So now that we were out of school for the summer, I figured we could talk all night, and I could sleep all day! We had been together since April, and for twelve-year-olds, that was the equivalent of twenty years. He was different though. He was born in the South and had only been in Detroit for three years. We got to know each other because he hung out a lot at my house with my uncle. One day, my cousin said he liked me, and when I looked at him, he didn't object. I had no idea because I have always been oblivious when it comes to picking up clues and hints. However, this particular day, I saw him in a different way. I had never noticed how attractive he was. I even appreciated how protective he was about family. So just like that, we were together.

Well, getting back to June, we were going strong, or so I thought. One day, I went to the park with my cousin (I was giving her relationship advice, and she was twenty-five at that time), and when we arrived back in the neighborhood, there he was, grinning in the face of another girl. She was an unfamiliar face, but she was so pretty with long hair. It felt like someone had just drained all the blood out of my body. I never said a word to him, but my face spoke volumes. I was devastated. I have always loved hard. I went in the house. I was so embarrassed. How could he do this right out in the open? He didn't even care if I saw him! I was so hurt. I just laid in the bed and cried.

After what felt like a lifetime, but was only an hour, I got up, grabbed his hat and necklace, and walked around to his house. He was sitting on the stoop. I asked him for my hat and necklace, and we swapped items and didn't say anything further. Just like that, it was over. Well, not really because I was vengeful and decided that I would make him feel the same way by getting someone BETTER than him.

Fast forward five years later, I was on the brink of adulthood and STILL had not given anyone else a chance because they weren't BETTER than my first love from five years prior. See, you don't understand. He was sun kissed and muscular with beautiful hair and a quiet, calming soul. Now, I didn't understand this at twelve, but I knew that whatever he had, the others didn't. As a result, I was still a virgin because no one fit the bill, and I wasn't about to give him my virginity because of how bad he hurt me. On one hand, it was good that I was still a virgin, but on the other hand, the reason was toxic.

Then one day it happened. I met him. The one that was BETTER than my ex. The one who would redeem my embarrassment and hurt. He was older, tall, handsome, and had beautiful hair. There was something about his eyes that intrigued me, and the major difference between him and my first love is that my new love didn't have a quiet, calming soul. In fact, his soul was raging, and at times, mysterious, but for some reason, I felt as if he would protect me. Oh, and he was worth the wait because when everyone saw us together, they would know that he was better than my ex.

Now, did you notice that I never talked about the character of the new guy? I wasn't even concerned with character. I guess many of us aren't at seventeen years old. However, we carry this practice well into adulthood, and after getting attached to the guy and letting him sample our goodies, we realize that he was no better than our ex. Further, if we want to make better choices, we should be focused on the man's connection with God, his leadership abilities, how he interacts with your children (and his), who he admires, how he handles conflict and how he complements your life. Instead, we often focus on who looks the best, has the best body, dresses the best, has the most money, is the most popular, and so on. When we break up with someone, there is a part of us that can't wait to see our replacement, and if they are ugly, funny built, broke, tangle-eyed, or have messed up teeth, it's OVER! Your swag will have just hit a million because she is NOT better than you. In my case, though, the girl that my first love replaced me with was beautiful, so I had to level up, but the question is, did I really?

Lastly, our trust issues are fueled by titles. Let me explain. See, when a person holds a title such as mother, father, sister, boyfriend, girlfriend, and even pastor, we expect them to perform in a certain way. We expect our mothers to be nurturing and to have a certain level of innocence. Our fathers are expected to be protectors and providers. We expect our boyfriends and girlfriends to be faithful, and our pastors to be godly and full of integrity. Correct? Well, what happens when our mothers are overwhelmed, overworked, and bitter, our fathers are absent, our boyfriends or girlfriends are cheaters, and our pastor is corrupt? We generalize and become skeptical of others, especially when it is our mother or father that doesn't live up to what we expected of them.

Don't get me wrong, we should've expectations of people, but those expectations shouldn't be based on their titles, but their actions, even if it is a parent. Let's face it, some parents have been crippled as a result of their own childhoods, and some are just plain irresponsible. We must realize that everyone won't live up to the titles that they hold, so we must give them leeway to be human, adjusting our expectations, based on what they do. In fact, I truly believe that a person won't live up to any title that he doesn't accept. So even if it is your mother and father, if they don't accept that responsibility, there will be a relational breakdown. Then if we are disappointed, we must remember the person who disappointed you is not an example of how all of those who hold that title will act. I've heard so many women say that all men are dogs, when the truth is you have only been hurt by one or two. Further, if you keep attracting "men" who use and hurt you, maybe they are drawn to the toxic part of you?

Low Self Esteem/Self Confidence

Self-esteem and self-confidence are key when it comes to who we attract. Confidence is attractive. Even if you are intimidated by the confidence of another—I call that the "She Thinks She's All That Syndrome"—there is still an attraction there because you really admire her or want what she has for yourself.

What's ironic is that we don't respect doormats and "Yes Men". Yet for some reason, when we like someone, we believe that if we agree with everything that he says, laugh at all of his jokes, and don't rock the boat, he will like us. However, it's just as much of a turnoff to guys for us to be doormats as it is for us to see them as doormats!

Have you ever heard that the one who cheats or leaves, often moves on to another relationship, while the one who was wounded or left, remains single? While times and tides are changing, women are typically the ones that are wounded and remain single after the heartbreak. But why would she remain single? Well, the most common reason is DAMAGED DATING! See, it's not that she doesn't meet anyone new. She probably has a whole list of guys that have been waiting for dude to mess up because for some reason, guys always wait until we're in a relationship to confess their love for us. So, after a pep talk from her sisters, cousins, or girls, she enters the "DAMAGED DATING PHASE." This is where she will act as if she is over the previous relationship but will work overtime to ensure that the same thing doesn't happen again. Thus, she finds herself cooking extravagant meals, entertaining guests, paying the bills, allowing him to move into her home with nothing to contribute, and other forms of behavior that are out of her character. She wants to be perfect, so she is not rejected again, and guess what happens; he leaves or misuses her too. Why? Well, our vibe attracts our tribe, and when we step out of character, we aren't being who we were designed to be. Therefore, the person that we attract is good for our "representative" who is the person that we portray, but when time reveals who we really are, there is a breakdown in the relationship.

All of this comes from one thing—when your ex broke your heart, he left you thinking that there was something wrong with you. If you take nothing else from this book, please know that while we all have areas that need improvement, he very well could have left because he wasn't ready for you! Remember, what we think of ourselves, good or bad, will manifest in our actions, and our actions will impact our relationships. So, if you enter a relationship believing that you aren't enough, you won't be.

Low self-esteem and self-confidence are also root causes of jealousy. You begin to think that your mate couldn't possibly be faithful to you because no one else has been or because of your past or shortcomings. Then the accusations start, and then, you are going through cell phones, pockets, wallets, and following him to see if work is really where he is going. When you don't think that you are enough for someone, you will always doubt their commitment to you, be it lover or friend. Sometimes, you will doubt the commitment so much that you will cheat first. Why? Because you know what it feels like to have your heart ripped into shreds and you refuse to be on the receiving end of that pain again.

Pride

I grew up hearing that pride comes before destruction. I had no idea what that meant, but I learned quickly. I was very competitive growing up. I mean, I hated to lose, and I still struggle with this—don't judge me. One day, I lost the eighth-grade spelling bee because of the word diesel. I had won every grade-level and school spelling bee that I had competed in from the fifth through the eighth grade. When I lost, it seemed like the whole school found out INSTANTLY! I was crushed, so much that I didn't come to school the next day. I really wished that I could be homeschooled because I didn't want to go back.

I went back and guess what was waiting for me, that humiliation of losing. The stares, whispers, laughs, and "you're still a winner in my eyes" pep talks. Even though I was a child, I had fallen into the vicious cycle of trying to live up to the hype. I had won so much until the teachers and principals started believing that I couldn't lose. Some of my classmates couldn't stand me and cheered against me because I was winning so much, even though I wasn't the type to brag. So, I felt as if I had to win because that is what was expected of me, and I didn't want to let down those who were supporting me. Losing was foreign for me, so I was terrified of the uncertainty that came with it. Would I keep losing? Would my supporters no longer support me? Did I fail?

You are probably saying what does pride and the spelling bee have to do with my relationship. Well, I carried that perfectionist mindset into adulthood. So, if I even perceived failure, my first instinct was to hide like I did when I misspelled diesel. This is what happens to us when we have been cheated on, beat on, lied to, or just failed altogether. If we can hide the situation, we will. If the situation happened publicly, we go into hiding. Why? Pride will make you try to live up to the hype. You know, the unrealistic expectations of others—the same people who don't have to deal with the consequences of your situation. You know what I mean right? Imagine this…You've been with your man for a couple of years, he treats you well, and you start giving others advice. Then he gets caught cheating. Well, you can't let them know that while you were giving out advice, your own relationship was being infiltrated. I mean, you have all the answers and your relationship was the standard that they were following, right? Yes, your relationship was perfect just like I was in the spelling bee. Yet here is the thing, no matter how well we perform, perfection is an illusion, and we must demand room to be human and not fall prey to having the infamous IMAGE.

How long will you hide the bruises and black eyes? How long will you grieve over a relationship that died long ago? How long will you make excuses for someone who is not even making excuses for himself? Let me guess, you have the Slot Machine Syndrome. Oh yes, you refuse to get up from the slot machine after years of losing and let the next one sit there and win. Sure, people change, and anything is possible, but in most cases, if you have been with him for years and he is not treating you well, you won't win, no matter how long you sit in that relationship.

We can't be too proud to cut ourselves loose from the thing that is killing or draining us. You can't be too proud to admit that you got it wrong, no matter how long you have gotten it wrong. I spent twenty years hoping that a man would get it together, and he never got it together for me. I struggled because love was the first ugly thing that I couldn't control. See, I lost the eighth-grade spelling bee, but I went back and won the school spelling bee that same year. So, in my eyes, I rebounded from that loss. Love, on the other hand, wasn't as simple. I was supposed to marry my first love and have a family with him. It was supposed to be a beautiful love story, except I wasn't the only one writing the script.

Pride made me focus on what it should've been and provided a beautifully-wrapped gift of false hope that eventually, things would line up with what Should've been! However, one day, I admitted that I got it wrong and decided that my pain would serve me well. Hence, you are reading this book. It's never too late to change directions, but pride will make you sit at a table where love is no longer being served. When will you realize that you are sitting at the table alone?

Selfishness

If you watch a baby, it doesn't take long for him to exhibit selfishness from not sharing his/her bottle to wanting mommy all to himself/herself. I believe that from that point on, we battle selfishness; some just have more of a battle than others. In other words, we all have a weak area that tempts us to be selfish, whether it's money, food, women/men, attention, etc., and when we enter a relationship, we take that weakness with us. Even if we make a conscious effort not to be selfish, we will always be tempted in our weak area.

Unfortunately, some of us have multiple weaknesses. I call them Takers. Takers rarely ever find other Takers to get with. They find Givers to get with instead. This can go one of two ways. Either the Giver and Taker balances one another, meaning the Taker helps the Giver to establish healthy boundaries in giving, and the Giver helps the Taker to be more generous; or the Taker can capitalize on the Giver's nature; thus, depleting the Giver. When the latter happens, and the Giver is depleted, one of the following occurs:

1) The Giver's heart hardens, and she becomes bitter. You've seen it before. In the beginning of the relationship, she was so happy to accept his multiple children, the fact that he had a criminal record, and was in between jobs or whatever the situation was. Then a year or two later, you see her on the brink of a nervous breakdown because she is carrying the whole load, or he got on his feet and left. Then, she resolves that she will never be there for another man in that way again. Sadly, this sets the next man up to pay for the sins of the previous man. As the old saying goes, "We often bleed on the one who didn't cut us."

2) The Giver will catch on and begin to create defense mechanisms to protect herself. This behavior ranges from hiding car keys to stashing money in hidden bank accounts and acting as if you have no money. You may think she has a reason to behave this way, and she is smart for protecting herself. However, this is unhealthy, as you shouldn't have to hide anything in a relationship. Unfortunately, hiding things have become so common that some of our mates have no idea who we really are, what we really like, or what we possess. This contributes to an atmosphere of distrust.

CHAPTER 3: WARNING SIGNS

I was taught that time reveals <u>all</u> things! What this tells us is that there are <u>always</u> warning signs of toxic relationships; it's just up to us to pay attention. Yet there are three major reasons that we miss the signs of a toxic relationship. First, some of us have been surrounded by toxicity for so long, that we think it's normal. We have seen our family members involved in the same types of fruitless relationships, so we tend to gravitate to what is "normal."

Then after years of living a nightmare, it is hard for us to accept that there were other options. In fact, in many cases, we may have rejected the other options because we tend to reject the unfamiliar. We've all heard stories of the one that got away. You know, it was the good guy that loved you, but you didn't understand their concept of love because it was pure and healthy. There was no drama or strings attached. He just loved you for you, and because you were so used to foolishness, you rejected it and filed it under the category of "TOO GOOD TO BE TRUE!" However, it was true and healthy, but because you had never seen anything like it, you passed and settled for what was "normal."

Another major reason that we miss signs of a toxic relationship is because we settle for the sake of having someone, believing that things will get better after the person sees how great we are or how much we have to offer. Sometimes, our pride just gets in the way, and we don't want to admit that we have desperately rushed into situationships because we didn't want to be alone or we were using our new guy to fill a void that he never had the ability to fill. Unfortunately, our society frowns upon those who are single and refuse to settle, almost as if they have some type of plague. Yet being alone doesn't mean lonely. In fact, time alone can be well spent if we use it for personal development. Besides, it is better to be single and happy than to be attached, lonely, and miserable. Contrary to what many may believe, relationships don't make you happy. You should already be happy when the opportunity presents itself.

Finally, we miss signs of a toxic relationship because we don't abstain from sexual relations long enough. Yes, I said it! We give "IT" up too quick. Sex clouds our vision. Soul ties and Sexually Transmitted Spirits are REAL! By the time we realize that we have been hoodwinked and bamboozled, some of us have exposed ourselves to enough ties and spirits to leave us bound for years! Then resentment sets in. We are frustrated because here we are again, doing the same dance to a different song. In some instances, we blame God for allowing this person to come into our lives, but did we really handle things God's way?

> *When I found out that there was another woman*
> *pregnant, I was devastated! Then to find out WHO*

was pregnant, I really wanted to wake up from the nightmare. See, I had met him when I was a young virgin. While I was mature for my age, I was still a nerd in high school, and he was out in the streets doing HIM! The night we met, he was drawn to me, even though I was quiet and shy. I smiled but never said much. After he left, I told my cousin that he was cute, and that "somehow" got back to him. When I saw him the next day, we talked and connected instantly. We talked all night while I played in his hair. He told me everything that he had done wrong, and I was thinking, "What if my father was a federal agent?" He didn't care. He poured his heart out as if he had been waiting for the opportunity to release his burdens. After that day, he kept visiting me, and one day, we were on my grandmother's porch, and out of the alley walks a girl. When he saw her, he yelled at her and told her to go back to the house. He kept talking as if nothing happened, and I stopped him and asked, "Who was that?" He told me that she was a girl that his great-aunt had taken in—where he was also staying. I asked why he spoke to her like that. He said that she had no business coming to my grandmother's house to look for him. I didn't question it for a few reasons, 1) It was Easter break, and I figured this "crush" would not go further because of the huge difference in the lives that we were leading, and 2) he wasn't my man and would never treat me like that. YEAH RIGHT!

School had always been what I needed to get back on track. I figured I would be back to normal on Monday morning and on to the next guy for summer break. I found myself in class daydreaming and wondering if he was thinking of me too. What was happening to me? I had to shake this. I had to shake him! I've always been stubborn, so I refused to call him. I told myself that it could never happen, and if you rehearse something long enough, you'll believe it. After two days, it worked, and just when I thought I was over him, my pager went off. I was so geeked because I had my answer. He was thinking of me too! We talked for about two weeks, and then I didn't hear from him again. I was back to square one. I told myself that it was fun while it lasted, and just when I was back in the swing of things, he called my house. I never gave him—or anyone—the number to my house because we never kept a phone line long enough for me to do so. I soon found out that he found my cousin (who originally connected us) and had her to call me because he had lost my pager number. I had never had anyone to pursue me that way. Surely, he would not want to waste my time, right?

We talked for the next couple of months. I met his family, and he met more of my family. We still had not been intimate, but we had fun together, talked a lot, and had so much in common. Then he suffered a devastating loss, and I didn't hear from him for a while. He tracked me down again, but this time, he came to see me and told me that he had met someone, and they were together. My heart skipped a beat, but I figured someone was satisfying his needs because I knew that I wasn't. She was older and was able to do things that I couldn't and wouldn't do. I wasn't ready to give up my virginity, and I was too young to play house. He, on the other hand, was grown. So, when he left this time, I resolved that my chapter with him was done. I was WRONG!

KILLER CONNECTIONS

My cousin met his brother, and they started "going together." She would come back and tell me that HE asked about me. She would also talk about his girlfriend and how he didn't really like her. I dismissed it because I figured she was just trying to cheer me up. I mean, I had a few new candidates, but none of them took my mind off HIM! I wouldn't admit it though. Then the date came.

I was the last one of my crew of cousins and friends to have sex because I was waiting for November 1995. See, I had seen a young lady graduate from high school pregnant, and I didn't want that for myself. So, I figured that if I didn't have sex until November or after, I would be good. Oh, how I wish my goals were more advanced, like waiting for marriage, but it's the past. I decided that I wanted to break my virginity, and I chose HIM to do it. I sent a message to him through my cousin, and he agreed to meet me. We met up on November 13, 1995. I was ready. I had a washcloth, soap, a Summer's Eve wet nap, and a sanitary napkin. I had waited all my years for this, and when I saw him, I was ready to get to it. He smiled so hard, kissed me, and just kept hugging me and telling me that he missed me. He had the music and room all ready. Finally, we got to it, and when I left that room and house, my innocence was gone... just like that.

I didn't really feel different. I mean, I was a little sore, but otherwise, I felt the same. I came home, called my mother and told her that I had been sexually active. She had always told me to let her know, and I kept my word. Then I thought about what my next move was. See, he and I agreed, since he had a girlfriend, that he would break my virginity, and we would never speak again. I truly believed that we would keep this agreement. Then the phone rang, and it was him. The agreement was scrapped, but I wasn't cool with him having a girlfriend, so I continued to talk to other guys. Then he called one day and said, "I can't handle you being with anyone else." RED FLAG! I mean, he had a WHOLE girlfriend at home, telling me that he needed me to be exclusive. I asked him what he planned to do with her. He said he would figure it out. So, while he was figuring it out, I was still going out with other dudes, but I reserved sex for him only. This continued for a year, and then he said he wanted to move in together and take our relationship to the next level. So, I fully committed, and I thought he had too, until he started staying out all night, and I found out that the girlfriend that he never broke up with was just as pregnant as I was.

When the Bible refers to sex, it uses the word "knew." Knew is the past tense of know, which means to develop a relationship with by spending time to become familiar with the person, place, or thing. So, by the time marriage and sex ensues, we should KNOW the person that we are allowing to access our body, soul, and spirit. This takes time, which reveals all things. See, it all really does come full circle. However, at 18 years old, I didn't want to hear any of this. I was in love, so I gave him full access to me. He was handsome and made me feel protected, but as I stood by that tree, confused as to how a misunderstanding had led to him hitting me, I suddenly felt as if I needed protection from the one who had once made me feel safe.

CHAPTER 4: MIND YA MIND

In my view, everything starts in/with the mind. Although we may believe that we don't THINK before we speak or act, it takes brain function to speak or act at all. With this theory in mind, I believe that before we ever enter a toxic relationship or exhibit toxic behavior, we possess a toxic mind. I've heard a toxic mind referred to as "Stinking Thinking." Either way, if we detox our mind, eventually our actions will follow. Sounds easy right? No, it's not exactly as easy as it sounds!

When you have a toxic mind, toxicity is the norm for you until your mind is exposed to something different AND accepts better as a possibility for you. Initially, I thought that people only needed to be exposed to something better to want better for themselves, but I soon realized that some people have endured so much that they may view something as being better but never see themselves as a worthy candidate for that life, love, or achievement. I'm here to tell you that YOU ARE WORTHY of a healthy relationship, but a toxic mind will cause you to forfeit it.

Normalizing dysfunction is dangerous because in that state of mind, you tend to cling to others with the same mindset. So, who will challenge you to live at a higher level if no one is mentally healthy enough to identify the areas in which you need to be more accountable? Therefore, it is important not to be the sharpest knife in the drawer because at some point in your life, you will need someone to hold you accountable and give you some level of correction too. So, let's discuss some toxic mindsets that may be stopping you from being your best and attracting God's best.

Toxic Mindset #1: Insecurity

Insecurity is usually buried. No, not because it is dead, but because it is the culprit that most people never dig deep enough to resolve. Think about it. You meet a guy, and all he does is brag about himself or what he has. You liked him or who you thought he was, until the façade was revealed. The first thing that someone will say is that he is bragging because he has never had anything— and that could be part of it—but if we dig just a little bit deeper, you will find that not only is he bragging because he is not used to the level of riches or power that he has, but he also feels as if those are the things that will keep you because HE is not enough. People that hide behind their wealth, power, or perceived success typically have deep-rooted issues with insecurity, and should they lose these things, they will become someone totally different because their confidence was fully invested in what they had or could provide, not in who they really are.

Unfortunately, insecurity never comes alone. You know what they say, "Misery loves company," right? When people lose confidence, insecurity shows up in the form of depression, cheating, immaturity, overreacting, jealousy, bragging, competition, and/or low self-esteem. We just never dig deep enough to know what the real root is. One thing is for sure, if you never get to the root of the issue, it will continue to manifest itself in different ways. For example, you stay in the house so that he doesn't accuse you of other men, and then he says you're depressing. So, you decide to get out more, but you've gained weight from sitting in the house and you can't fit anything. Therefore, you start working out to avoid buying new clothes—to avoid another argument—and then he has a problem with that. He claims you are getting right to leave him. It's confusing, right? Exactly! Insecurity breeds confusion! It seems like no matter what you do, it isn't right, but the truth is, he's insecure and part of him may even wonder why you want him when there are so many others out there that are better than him. It's like fighting an invisible battle, and guess who loses?

Toxic Mindset #2: Jumping to Conclusions

GUILTY! Yes, I have done it. I will admit it. However, now that I have a healthier mindset, I take the proper steps to eliminate assumptions. By now, you may be able to assess that I like getting to the root of issues. So, when I look at why we really jump to conclusions, the first thing that comes to mind is emotions.

KILLER CONNECTIONS

Emotions were NEVER meant to lead us. They are just indicators that let us know when something is right or wrong. That's it! Emotions were never meant to be vehicles because they either lead us down dead-end streets, into ditches, or off cliffs. If you don't believe me, think back to the last time you jumped to a conclusion. Now, when the information that ruffled your feathers came along, were you already emotional about the situation? The person may have known that you were already bothered by it and added fuel to the fire. What did you do when you received the new information? Did you stop and think? Did you stop and consider the source? Did you take a minute to even process whether the information made sense? I'm willing to bet that you didn't stop and think. You immediately acted, even if that means pacing the floor and talking yourself angry. That is all fueled by emotion.

After all the huffing and puffing, talking and walking, and crying and sighing, you take your concocted story to the source and find out that there was a misunderstanding, or it was a flat-out lie. For instance, the girl that your messy friend saw in his car was really his cousin from out of town that was here for the family reunion, or the piece of the conversation that your messy friend brought you meant something totally different when it was placed in full context. Now, understand, I'm not telling you that your friend might not come with good information from time to time. After all, that is why you still believe her, right? However, what

I'm saying is if you profess to be an adult, then you must hold yourself to the standard of what adults do. Either take the information, sit on it, and observe or go to the source and address your concerns. Yet if you aren't prepared to do anything, you might not want to say anything because what you allow will continue.

Further, acknowledging poor behavior but not addressing it by establishing boundaries, for example, only results in him having less respect and more resentment towards you. I remember watching G.I. Joe when I was younger. Their slogan was "Knowing is half the battle." So, when someone brings you information about your relationships, one of the first questions needs to be, "What am I willing to DO about this?" If the answer is nothing, then that is also what you should say, as men tend to respond to actions, not words.

Toxic Mindset #3: Overgeneralizing

I've heard "all men" statements for many years. As an inquisitive and logical child, I wondered if the women had been with every man to make these statements. As I grew older, I realized that we make these overgeneralized statements from their limited views, and unconsciously, I was no different.

I remember my mother saying that she would never date a man with double L's in his name because she had children by a

KILLER CONNECTIONS

William (first name) and a Williams (last name). Then I found myself saying that I would not deal with any man whose name began with an R. I'm laughing as I write this because I said it the other day out of habit. These are overgeneralizations, and if we aren't careful, they will become superstitions that we allow to govern our lives. Every man whose name starts with an R is not a bad man. I haven't even met every man whose name starts with an R, just as my mother hasn't met every man in the world who has double L's in his name. We simply had bad experiences and decided to side eye everyone that fit what we deemed as the commonalities between the men that had wasted our time.

How many times have you said that you would not date a man that was a specific astrological sign, born a certain year, that has a certain name or from a certain part of town because you had one or maybe two guys that had this certain thing in common and a relationship didn't work out between you and him? Sure, it seems safe to say and even to follow. However, the truth is that you are what you draw. Something in you attracted something in them, and if they were toxic, you were too. So if you keep attracting toxic people, no matter what their name, birthday, or location is, you are the REAL common denominator, and living by the superstitions that you have accepted into your heart—because it's easier than detoxing—can cause you to miss the person for whom you may be praying.

Toxic Mindset #4: Competition

Theodore Roosevelt said that *Competition is the thief of joy.* Apparently, I didn't believe him, and before you laugh, you didn't either. His statement, however, is so true for a few reasons. First, competition will lead you to be with someone that you don't want to be with, buy things you don't like, go places that you don't want to be, and partake in activities that aren't satisfying, all because you are competing with someone who may not even know that you are in competition with them. How silly is that?

Many of us have wasted years competing with our siblings, our man's ex, our ex's new woman, a side chick, classmates, and so on just to make a point that we are better. My question to you is, better at what? We all have our lanes in which we excel, but none of those lanes require us to compete for our success. You are TOO UNIQUE TO COMPETE, but you need to know that for yourself. There is something that you can do, that you sibling can't. If you are with the man now, there is something that he saw in you that he didn't see in his ex. If you are in competition with the ex's new woman, like I was, STOP! I checked myself so hard, not because I'm better than her, but because I'm better than THAT! Competing with her won't change the situation, but competition at that level will lead you to compromise. This is how so many men get away with sleeping with multiple women while they all know about one another. They are competing and not holding him responsible or accountable.

Speaking of which, competition causes us to remain in situations that aren't serving us well for much longer than we should remain. If we are honest, we don't even want him or whatever we are in competition over. We just want to beat the other person. If you are anything like I was, you are holding on because you refuse to let her beat you. Yet what happens if you end up with him? Will you be happy? Often, we aren't happy with the person that he is now. The person that we loved is long gone, and if we end up with who he is now, especially seeing as though you all are in a love triangle or quad, you will be miserable. Is that really winning?

Lastly, competition causes us to stray from our destiny. How? Well, if you are in competition with someone, you are watching them closely, right? Therefore, you aren't watching the one with the playbook. Focusing on your opponent means that you are allowing their moves to dictate your moves, and eventually, you will compromise the directives that God may give you. I once asked a question, "If your enemy had the answer to your problem, how long would you have the problem." Most people didn't touch the question, I gather, because it would not have been consistent with the messages that they preach. However, one young lady was honest and said she would have the problem forever. Well, when it comes to mindset, our competition is the equivalent of an enemy.

Think about it. If you are in competition with your mate, you are sleeping with the enemy. You are withholding ideas that could make him better because you want to be better than or smarter than him. If you are in competition with your sibling, you were raised and have lived with the enemy. You aren't looking out for his or her best interest like a sister does, but instead, you are watching and waiting for him or her to fail so you can triumph. Why? Because you want to show your husband that you are his equal. Because your mother or father favored your sibling growing up.

Unfortunately, the competition doesn't stop there. We now have mothers and daughters/fathers and sons competing right in the home. How can you properly parent a child when you don't want the best for them? As a parent, you should wish for your child to achieve more in life than you did. However, competition will make you compromise what you know is right because you want to win and show them up! Sadly, as you "win" the competition, you will find out that in most cases there is no "them" because you were in competition by yourself.

CHAPTER 5: CHECK YASELF!

I know that we have discussed toxic relationships, for the most part on a more intimate level, but relationships with family members and friends can be toxic as well. In Chapter Three, we discussed four major areas (communication, trust, time, and respect) that help us to evaluate the health of our relationships. In this chapter, we will take our evaluation a step further by reviewing specific traits that prove that our relationships are toxic. Brace yourself!

Trait One: Manipulation

Manipulation reveals itself in many forms within a toxic relationship. Whether he uses your weaknesses and secrets against you, invokes pity after doing wrong, throws a tantrum and withholds something as a result of not getting his way, turns the situation around to blame you or capitalizes on your emotions by crying when he has been "caught up," it's all manipulation! Oh, and one more thing, it's TOXIC! I'm sure those things were expected to be listed under manipulation, but what about the one who always quits the relationship? You guessed right, it's toxic, and guess what, I've been guilty of that a time or two myself. When we are angry and frustrated, it is easier to quit instead of arguing, but if you find that quitting becomes the go-to solution for either of you, it's toxic! Why? Well, relationships are supposed to be secure. So how can there be security when the other party is subject to bail on you whenever they feel "some type of way?" Relationships should be secure enough to reserve quitting as a last resort, and in some cases, quitting may not be an option at all.

Oh, but wait, there's more! Did you know that it is also manipulative to withhold sexual relations from your husband, especially when you are doing it because you are upset or trying to get what you want? Biblically, when you are joined together as one, your body belongs to your spouse, and vice versa. As a matter of fact, even if you plan to fast, you are instructed to first get permission from your spouse because typically fasting includes sexual abstinence. Therefore, sex is not be used as a weapon. Now, ladies before you get upset and close the book, please note that the same can be said for money. If your man is the breadwinner and he withholds money because he is upset and wants to punish you, that's just as toxic!

Lastly, it's also manipulative to be too clingy. Let me explain. When you first got together, you couldn't get enough of each other. Your friends were wondering who this person was that had you so intrigued that you willingly missed out on your regular social activities. Everything was great, the jokes were funny, and you even hated to go to work without him. However, after the newness of the relationship wore off, it wasn't cute anymore. Now, he wants all your time and attention and finds any reason to have issues with your friends and in some cases, your family. You already know what I'm going to say... TOXIC! Why? Every relationship should involve "me time" for each party and a certain level of trust and assurance, during that time, that he will remain committed. Isolation is not a sign of a healthy relationship, and usually, the person that desires all your time, has suffered with fear of abandonment (as we discussed earlier) and needs to get healed.

Since I have told you what's toxic about manipulation, let me tell you what the alternatives are, COMPROMISE and HARMONY! There should be times when each party sacrifices for the stability of the relationship. Notice I said harmony and not balance. In my view, when I think of balance, I think of a scale. A scale only balances when both sides have an equal amount of weight. Remember what I said earlier about that Teddy Pendergrass song? Equal responsibility and compromise are ideal, but oftentimes that doesn't happen. Scales become unbalanced when one side bears too much weight. However, relationships can very well maintain harmony when one party is bearing more than the other, if the party is not left bearing more on a permanent basis.

Trait Two: Jealousy/Obsession

In the previous section, we talked about the perils of being too clingy. This section takes it a step further. Let's be honest, you love for your man to make a fuss over you at times. I know I do. It makes me feel wanted, special, and warm all on the inside. However, when this happens continuously, it becomes overwhelming. First, you have to call and check in all the time because he needs constant reassurance that you are still committed. Then the one time you are in a meeting, class, or you are just unable to answer the phone, the accusations start. Then you're on trial, and you've never even cheated or talked to another person!

Let me pause for a quick disclaimer. Please note that it is understandable that you may have to provide reassurance after you have cheated or been found guilty of some level of indiscretion, as trust takes time to rebuild. However, providing reassurance only works when the wounded party is willing to trust again. If not, it is just wasted time and energy because the indiscretion will always be a factor in some way or another, and it will probably be thrown in your face, continuously.

Okay, let's get back to your trial. So, you now walk on egg shells because he has conjured up a conspiracy in his mind as to why you didn't answer your cell phone, or why you didn't call on your break. I lived this for many years. I worked seven days per week, attended college part time, and with the time I had left, I spent it with my mate and my daughter, and I was STILL accused of cheating to the point where he went through my cellular phone because he was trying to catch me up. I was always taught that the person who is accusing is often the one cheating. So, when everything came to the light, I realized that he was looking for something to justify his wrongdoing. Nonetheless, it was stressful and—you guessed it—TOXIC! There is no purity in insecurity!

Furthermore, jealousy and obsession are fear based. The person often believes that you will leave them like someone else did, or he believes that a more-fitting person will come along and become the apple of your eye. Either way, this is fear of abandonment that manifests as jealousy, and it is not healthy.

I was five months pregnant when I found out I wasn't the only one pregnant. To make matters worse, we were set to deliver around the same time. As usual, he denied it at first, but then he came clean about the situation. I felt stuck. After finding out about the other baby, I decided that I wanted to move on, but move on to who? Where? He was all that I knew. I met someone, and we talked on the phone for a while. Then he wanted to see me. So, I would meet him at my aunt's house, and one day, he noticed that it was hard for me to climb into his truck. I have never been a good liar, so I told him that my stomach was bothering me. After he left, I cried because I knew that I had to tell him. He liked me, and soon, he would want to take things to an intimate level, and I could NEVER be pregnant with one man's child and lay with another man. Two weeks later, I told him the truth, and he was so hurt that he hung up, and I didn't speak to him until years later. After telling him that, I just remained alone until I reconciled with my mate. By that time, it was almost time for both babies to be born.

He got the call one morning that his baby was coming. We were doing well at the time, so he was so nervous that I was going to flip out on him. I mean, I was nine months pregnant dealing with him having another child. He was my first in so many areas, but I wasn't his first in anything, not even the first to have his child. However, I told him that I forgave him, and I didn't go back on my word. I could tell forgiveness was foreign to him because he called me so many times from that hospital that he irritated me. When the baby was finally born, he called to tell me, and I could hear the happiness and sadness in his voice. He was happy that he was a father but sad because he knew that no matter how much I said that I was okay, I really wasn't. My heart was torn to pieces.

Three weeks later, on my due date, my contractions were five minutes apart, but my water hadn't broken. He drove me to the hospital, and sure enough, I had dilated six centimeters. I had the baby that day, in the same hospital that he had become a father just three weeks prior. I heard one of the nurses tell him that he looked familiar. My heart skipped a beat, but I never said a word. After having the baby, I poured myself into school and work, and guess what? Despite all that he had put me through, he was still jealous! He was jealous of how much time I spent at work. If I missed his call, there were questions and sometimes accusations.

One time, I had been working, attending night classes, and whatever time I had left, belonged to my baby, so my aunt suggested a weekend trip to see my best friend. I agreed. Whenever I was around my best friend, we had fun. I needed that fun because I was young but living the life of a forty-year-old woman. Every year, my best friend had a pajama party during Super Bowl weekend, giving the ladies something to do while their men were absorbed with the game. So, I decided that I would take my weekend trip on Super Bowl weekend. Now, my mate and I had been on and off because he was up to the usual foolishness. So, when I reserved my car and made these plans, we were on a "break". When we got back together, and I told him about it, he played nice. When I pulled up in that rental car, the drama started. He showed out until I said the magic words: Do you want to go? I didn't mind him going because I didn't have anything to hide, but I didn't expect him to say yes because he really didn't like my best friend. He said yes, and his brother decided to go with him, so I thought he would be cool.

The plan was for me to go to the pajama party and he would chill with his brother at a nearby hotel. When we got there, I called my best friend and asked her to show me where the hotel was. Keep in mind, this was before the GPS era. She said that she had a house full, but she would send someone to ride with me. She sent her neighbor, who I was cool with, to guide us to the hotel. When she got in the car, she started talking about how wild they were at the pajama party. Now, I had been to the annual pajama party before, and we had fun, but it wasn't quite what she was describing. What I didn't understand was why she chose to tell me about the party in front of my man? I could see the tips of his nose flaring up like a bull, and I had not done anything, nor did I even know any of the guys she had named.

As soon as I closed the door of the car and was out of ear shot of everyone in the car (my best friend's neighbor and his brother), he went OFF! He questioned me about who I was supposed to meet there and went on and on. He told me that I wasn't going back over there that night. So, I rented the two rooms; one for his brother, and one for us thinking that he would chill out by the next day. He rode with me to drop my best friend's neighbor off, so I made up an excuse about being tired from the drive and said that I would see them in the morning.

We woke up to the sound of my best friend's ringtone. I already knew what she was calling for. Saturday morning breakfast was part of the pajama-party itinerary. I answered the phone, and when I looked over at him, I could tell that it wasn't a good idea for me to leave. So, I made up another excuse and said that I just wanted to have breakfast with my man and would get with the ladies for fun later. We went to breakfast in the hotel lobby, cracked jokes, and had fun. I was thinking that he was easing up. After breakfast, I went back to our room for a nap, and he went to his brother's room. He saw a car leave that was like the one I had rented. He came bursting through the door, breathing hard, and I was looking at him like he was crazy. He said, "Oh, I thought you had left."

Since he had interrupted my nap, we watched television for a while. The whole time, I was thinking of a great escape, so I could be with my friends. I mean, that was the whole purpose of me coming to visit! I was so aggravated. Then I had what I thought was a great idea. If we were intimate, he would relax because then he would know that I wasn't going to be intimate with anyone else. So, it went down, and again, we woke up to the sound of my best friend's ringtone. This time, I told her that I would be there after I got myself together. He seemed like he was okay with me leaving. I got dressed and even called while I was driving over to her place. When we got off the telephone, he said that he was going to sleep, and I told him that before we went out that night, I would come back to the hotel to take them—him and his brother—to get some food. He said okay.

Of course, I got clowned when I got there. The ladies teased me for being on lockdown. About three hours later, we were having fun and helping each other get ready to go out. Just as I was telling my best friend that I had to go back to the hotel to take my mate and his brother to get some food and to change my clothes, my phone rang. When I answered the phone, all I heard was yelling! "YOU JUST GONE LEAVE US HERE HUNGRY HUH?" I left, and when I got to the hotel, he wouldn't answer the phone or come downstairs. His brother came downstairs, and we rode to get something to eat. Then he called me all the way to and from the restaurant, arguing, and I was confused as to what his problem was.

When I got back to the hotel, I went in to calm him down and change my clothes. I sat and talked to him, but as I got dressed, the tension returned. He said that he was okay with me going but pouted the whole time. After my vibe was officially killed, I just called my best friend and told her that I wasn't going out because I really didn't like clubs. She knew he was the reason that I had changed my mind and started cursing and going off. I just told her that I would see her tomorrow and hung up. After he heard me say that I wasn't going, he said, "No, I want you to go." At this point, I wanted to drive back to Detroit and leave him right there. I had a terrible headache, and I needed a getaway after that getaway just to calm my nerves. After we got back to Detroit, he went to a Super Bowl party, and had the audacity to stay out all night, but I was so irritated that I didn't even care. His jealousy and obsession had ruined my trip, and I had let it.

KILLER CONNECTIONS

Unfortunately, it wouldn't be the last time that I would deal with it.

Most of the time, when we talk about jealousy, we talk about it from the aspect of intimate relationships. However, jealousy has torn families and friendships apart as well. For instance, when I found out I was pregnant, I was so confused because I thought he couldn't have children. Even his mother said that he was told at a young age that he would not have children. My baby is one of the best things that ever happened to me, but then, I was 18 years old, and I had just entered my freshman year of college on a scholarship, two months prior to getting pregnant. Immediately, many of my family members, or shall I say, relatives—because there is a difference—began to say things like, "We knew she wouldn't graduate from college!" That was so hurtful to me because I didn't understand why there was so much hate toward me, when I was raised to love family. I now understand that it was because of my relationship with my grandmother. They said that I was her favorite, and because of her love for me, I suffered a lot of resentment. Then it happened. I GRADUATED! I was the first in my family to graduate from college. Then I did it again, and this time, I presented my grandmother with my master's degree on her birthday as a gift.

As I continued to accomplish things despite obstacles, I faced jealousy from the very people that I thought would celebrate with me, even though I never used my accomplishments to belittle others. Hence, I learned—the hard way—that there is a very distinct difference between family and relatives. I share my life with family. I share blood with relatives. My family appreciates and celebrates me, and they may not be blood. My relatives may tolerate and associate with me when it benefits them. Understanding this, helped me to heal from the rejection that I had faced during my childhood.

As far as friends are concerned, jealousy rears its ugly head in these relationships too. First, we'll discuss the possessive friend. I have never been able to deal with this nonsense. This friend feels as if you are only supposed to have them as a friend. If you deal with others, she gets upset and start to act as if you are excluding her from your whole life. This is the friend who claps loud and hard for your accomplishments, but the whole time, she is looking around to make sure no one else is clapping harder than her.

This friend can be dangerous for a few reasons. First, God often uses divine connections to guide us along our path. How can you have divine connections when it will take a divine intervention for you to meet someone new because of this territorial friend that you have? Secondly, some possessive friends become so jealous and afraid of losing you as a friend that they may hurt you. I know you think that is extreme, and it is, but it has happened. Lastly, we need new relationships and experiences in our lives to grow, so if you <u>only</u> remain friends and keep company with this one friend, your maturity will be severely stunted.

In addition to the possessive friend, jealously also introduces the one-up friend. This friend is in competition with you, and you aren't aware of the competition or competing. Everything you do, she does it too or attempts to do it better. Whatever you wear, she wears it too or attempts to wear it better. Whomever you date, she has someone better or she is discouraging you! Unfortunately, you don't see it because you may have been friends for a long time or you really have love for her. Sometimes knowing a person's history will cause us to make excuses for their behavior, so you tell people that she is not really that bad because of that one heart-to-heart that you shared in the 12th grade. However, since that time, she has been gutting you, and there you stand, bleeding and telling everyone that all is well.

This friend is dangerous because she will pump you up to do crazy stuff, just so she can look better than you when you fail. Taking advice from or being vulnerable with this "frienemy" is the equivalent of taking sleeping pills in the bed with a starving python. I remember a young lady that would wait until there was a house full of guys and she would embarrass her friends. She would expose the friend who had borrowed her shirt. She would expose personal business about her friends, crack jokes on her friends and/or do anything that would get the guys' attention. Her friends would make excuses and attribute it to humor or her just having no filter. However, I didn't think it was very funny or cool to humiliate people that way, especially when she couldn't accept the same humiliation happening to her, and the people that she was hurting were supposed to be her friends. As a wise woman once said, *If the snake is sick or wounded, call and get it some help. Don't take it inside because wounded or not, a snake is out for itself.* Again, don't let a person's history give them a pass to exhibit toxic behavior.

Trait Three: Blaming & Vengeance

I think everyone has struggled with blaming and vengeance at some point in our lives. Some of us are still struggling with these traits now. It is so instinctive to pass the buck, especially when it is a tough situation that we would rather not deal with. Then there are cases where it is the other person's fault, but there were some things that we could have done differently. I know I've been guilty, and guess what… I didn't want to hear anything about what I could have done differently. It was all their fault, and I was going to get them back.

KILLER CONNECTIONS

When it came to blame and vengeance, I was one of the worst kinds. My blame game was trump tight because I would lay low and get facts. By the time I pleaded my case, I was in full effect like an attorney. I would have dates, times, locations, apparel details, and everything. It would be laid out so meticulously that I would win the arguments on presentation alone! Then when it came to revenge, I had that down to a science as well. I didn't care how long I would have to wait, how far I'd have to go, or how much I'd have to give or pay, I was going to strike when you least expected it. What made matters worse was the fact that I was okay with no one knowing that it was me who did it! See, most people get their kicks from letting everyone know that they got the person back to restore their image. I didn't care. As long as I knew, that was all that mattered. In fact, I thrived on being the innocent one who had been done wrong and never retaliated. Does that sound familiar? Well, you notice that everything there is past tense, right? Thank GOD for deliverance because I'm not that person anymore.

Both blaming and vengeance result from vision issues. When it comes to blaming, we tend to amplify what the accused has done, but we never stop to SEE what we could have done to change the outcome. One day, I was in a car accident. I was upset because my car was five days old. An older lady hit me, and the police said that it was my fault. Well, I felt as if it was her fault because she shouldn't have sped up when I was trying to get over! I never

79

thought about how I could have gotten in the appropriate lane in the beginning instead of waiting until the last minute, how I could have slowed up and allowed her to pass me, or how I could have just circled around after missing the turn. No, it was HER FAULT, and my beautiful, black Pontiac Grand Prix was damaged. I couldn't see it any other way.

See, the way in which you interact with the blaming process determines whether it will be hard for you to forgive. When we don't forgive, we jeopardize our own forgiveness from God as well as our own health. There are so many people walking around with weight from things that occurred decades ago. Why? Well, the first step of forgiveness, admitting your responsibility in the matter, can be the hardest step. It's so hard that some never even start the process. Now, there are some instances where you have no responsibility, such as being molested. In those cases, the first step to forgiveness is to release responsibility (victims often blame themselves).

Outside of those types of circumstances, it's simple. You can't blame and accept responsibility for the same thing at the same time. You must choose one and abandon the other. Unfortunately, most of the time, we choose to blame because it's easier. Blaming only passes the responsibility of the poor action, but many times, it falls to the ground because there is no one there to accept it. In other words, you may never get the apology or acknowledgement of the wrong that you are seeking. This causes you to withhold forgiveness, and unforgiveness leaves you with distorted vision, particularly in the area that you have been hurt.

When it comes to vengeance, I want you to think back to when I said that it didn't matter how long I had to wait, how far I had to go, or how much I had to give or pay, I would get the person back. This means that it consumed me, and rightfully so, because vengeance is God's job. It was the equivalent of a snake's actions. The snake never takes its eyes (VISION) off its prey. This means that when you are consumed with vengeance, you miss out on opportunities and lessons for growth and development. This is how a person remains at the same level in life for many years—a lack of focus in the proper areas. You can be so focused on getting revenge or waiting for that person to fail that you forget to live, love, and learn. The same is true for the person who blames others for their issues and/or remains saturated with unforgiveness until they receive an apology, that may never come. It simply leaves the person TOXIC!

Trait Four: Overreacting

If I asked why you overreact, you'd probably say that it is an emotional response to being provoked because, oh my goodness, we never start the fight or disagreements, right? Now, to some degree, this may be true. However, emotions would be the surface reason, not the root—and you know how I feel about getting to the root of things. Here's why.

Think about the last time you overreacted. Where did the emotions behind it all come from? I would say perceived disappointment, embarrassment, or shame. What were you disappointed, embarrassed, or ashamed of? Could it be that you went against the grain, believed in him, and he played you, for example? If so, then the real root is EXPECTATIONS. We often overreact because we thought things would be different, and when we realize the truth—i.e. he played you just like he played everyone else—we go OFF THE DEEP END!

Please don't feel condemned because we all have been there, and the only way that you get better with investing expectations is to use Godly wisdom and discernment. Even still, people will fail us. They will disappoint us. They will hurt us. We just need to decide if the relationship is worth fighting for. In the interim, it is not okay to act up, break out car windows, flatten tires, and call the police and get him locked up, especially when you are going to be the one fixing the windows, getting a new set of tires, and paying the bail.

Another issue with overreacting is with the fact that things often escalate, sometimes to the point of physical contact or even death. I've heard about it a million times. Here's just one scenario. A girl gets a call from a friend telling her that her man was riding a chick around. She is hurt because he swore that he would not cheat again. She can't look like a fool in front of her girls, so by the time she sees him, she is "38 hot." He comes in, getting ready to tell her that he reconnected with his cousin, and SLAP! She slaps him right across his face. Now, he's a little tipsy and caught off guard, so what does he do? SLAP! Now she is devastated because he hit her—never mind the fact that she hit him first. She goes wild on him, and he manages to leave. She is crying and calls her brothers, and now, we got action. This situation has taken a life of its own now, and sometimes, it gets REALLY, REALLY, ugly.

Please know that I don't condone violence in any way, tipsy or not. Further, this is just one scenario, and yes, I know that sometimes he is guilty, and the girl might not have been his cousin; but the point is, his woman expected one thing, and when she perceived something different, disappointment and hurt turned into an emotional rage, and it spilled over into the lives of others as many of our fits of rage usually do.

Sometimes, when he disappeared, it was a relief because I could work as much as I wanted. I had been waiting to work at this law firm since I was a child. I used to go to work with my mother, and all the people spoiled me. I got typing assignments, helped answer the phones, and they always let me choose the lunch spot. It was so fun there.

After I had my daughter, I prayed that God would bless me with a full-time job because I had sat in the Family Independence Agency (FIA) Office from 9 a.m. to 3 p.m. just to get Medicaid for my newborn baby—my mother's insurance covered me because I was still in college, but not my baby. When I left the FIA office that day, I knew I had to do something so that I would not be treated like crap after wasting so much of my time waiting for the FIA worker to call my name. They say that God doesn't hear a sinner's prayer. Well, I was living in sin, so some saint must have been praying with me because I received a call to work at the law office that I had dreamed of working for since I was eight or nine years old. The funny thing is, I never applied or told anyone that I was looking for a job.

I went to the interview, and someone else had been referred for the receptionist position for which I applied, but they interviewed me anyway since I was there. They took me to the Chief Executive

Officer's office for the last portion of the interview, and we had a talk. She said, "Hold on." She made a call and told a few people—members of her executive team—to come to her office. When they arrived, she asked me to repeat what I said to her. I repeated it. She told me to go out to the lobby, and they would be with me in a moment. Approximately twenty minutes later, they offered me a newly-created position in the executive suite as the administrative assistant for human resources and accounting. I made $6.97 per hour—I still have my first check stub—and in hindsight, that wasn't enough to live. However, I had full benefits for my baby, and because I had always been resourceful, I didn't care about the money. I called the FIA worker that same day and told her, "THANK YOU, but I don't need the benefits anymore."

My mother told me to learn as much as I could from the CEO and that if I took care of her, she would take care of me. I heeded to that wisdom. I would take my baby to work with me on the weekends. She had a ball on her blanket with her toys as her mother learned as much as she could from the Executive Secretary to the CEO. I did this for eight months, and then it happened. The Executive Secretary was leaving the agency in two weeks, and guess who knew her job... ME!

When I took over, I was terrified. I just knew I would get fired my first week. I think the fact that I made good coffee and didn't talk a lot helped me! Well, it was God's grace, but you know what I mean. I listened and learned. Then she told me that I could work whenever I wanted and gave me keys to the office. It was on then! I missed the whole summer of 1999. I would go in the office at 10 a.m. and leave at 10 p.m. Imagine the flack that I was getting when I got home. I didn't care though. I had a plan, and the funny thing is, money was never the main part of the plan. I gave most of that money away and ended up filing bankruptcy, but that's another story for another day. My plan was to learn everything I could from the CEO because that could never be taken away, and I did.

See, my mate and I had a conversation when we decided to make it official. He said that he wanted to own a specialty shop, and I said I wanted to help people as a psychologist. We both agreed that we would run our own practices because we would not allow others to dictate our dreams. I was and still am a very literal person, so after that conversation, I started working toward my part of the goals. He would work at times but seemed to be going in a different direction. It seemed like the closer to my dream that I came, the further away from him that I was. The countless hours working with the CEO was temporary, as those types of gravy trains always are, and it was a part of my plan. Meanwhile, he was busy trying to be "The Man" in the neighborhood, and that type of stuff just didn't interest me. We were growing apart, and I refused to accept it, but things started to happen that made me realize the hard truth.

It was a crisp, winter Saturday evening. My daughter, who had just turned two, and I were in the bed. I had not seen her father in a couple of days. I called his mother's house, and he wasn't there. Well, I have always been told that I missed my private investigator calling because I somehow ended up with a number for his other daughter's mother. You remember her, the one who delivered just three weeks before me. I called her, and she said that he wasn't there, but the funny thing is, about an hour later, he came bursting through the door with a few friends, telling my mother that she needed to "gone call the police" because he was about to put his hands on me. Now, timeout, didn't he say that wouldn't happen again? By now, it had happened twice. After the first incident at the college, he slapped me again because I wouldn't let him take my car to go and have a family day with his daughter and her mother. Yes, I said my car! He had gotten just that bold. Now do you see why disrespect can never be disregarded? Once again, he told me that it would never happen again. However, he was just a few feet away from me, but this time, things would be different.

As he came close to the room, I told him to "get on" because I didn't feel like it. He really got mad when he said something about me calling his daughter's mother, and I asked him how he knew that I had called her if he was in Jackson, Michigan like he claimed to be (she didn't live in Jackson, Michigan, by the way)? I guess he didn't expect me to figure that out, but the funny thing is, I knew about a lot of his indiscretions. I just believed he would grow up and realize I was the best thing that had happened to him. Well, he slapped me again as I was getting out of the bed with my baby. This time, I had something for him. I pushed him out of the room, and when he came back, I swung and connected twice. He pushed me, and I didn't want to fall on my baby, so I ended up in the closet, but all I could think was, "If I hit this floor, he might try to stump me." So, I grabbed his hair on my way down, and I beat the back of his head until my mother and his friends separated us. This time, I called the police, but I didn't press charges. Unfortunately, this wasn't our last fight.

Trait Five: No Progress Allowed

As I think back over the years, I have always been a "go-getter". Whether it was getting paid $50 per day to scream 5-0—thank GOD the police never came on my shift—babysitting or selling my aunt's condoms that she had gotten from the free clinic for 50 cents each, I always seemed to find a way to make money. This was partially because I hated depending on people. In my mind, if my mother had let me down, they would too. So outside of food, shelter, and a field trip or two, I didn't ask for or require too much from my grandmother or aunt. When you add this type of mentality to relationships, it can make waves. Why? Because most men have been taught to associate their manhood with the ability to financially provide for their families while neglecting the fact that sometimes women may not "need" a man's money to survive, but she will need his logic to bring harmony to her emotional relations.

The funny thing about my relationship is that he was torn when it came to my progress. On the day of my graduation, he caused me so much stress going back and forth about whether he would come. Then at the last minute, he said he would come, but I would have to come and get him. When I said that I wasn't sure if I could get my mother's car, make it to get him, and still be on time, he went into an emotional fit about how I didn't want him there. I picked him up and during the ride he apologized and told me how proud of me he was. I was happy he was there but wished he had made more of an effort to show how proud he was.

When it was time for me to go to college, he was proud but afraid. He used to tell me that I would find someone at college and not want him anymore. He had no idea that I wasn't even looking for anyone. This is part of the reason that he overreacted when he came into the college cafeteria and saw me joking around with my former high-school classmate—you remember when I was standing at the tree? That's when he started staying out all night. A year later, I received a job at a law office downtown. The accusations went from college guys to lawyers. He figured a lawyer would catch my eye and steal my heart, even though I came home to him EVERY night. So, when I excelled, he was proud, but afraid and threatened because he was reminded of the fact that we were growing apart, or as he said it, "You were outshining me." I had no idea we were in competition. I thought we were on the same team. Boy was I wrong.

Trait Six: Never Satisfied

As you read the real-life passages, you are probably like, "Why didn't you leave?" Well, first, I was young and thought he would change. Yet as I said previously—and it bears repeating, just in case you think you have the power to change him—people change for two reasons: a sense of loss or a sense of gain. After dealing with blatant disrespect in the form of babies, not coming home at night, and other women, he knew that I wasn't going anywhere. Another reason that I didn't leave is that all the times weren't bad. When we first got together, we didn't have an argument for a year and a half. We hung like wet clothes and had a ball. Through the years, we would have those times where we had so much fun, and it always seemed that those times came just when I was ready to give in. Isn't that something? So, it wasn't just back-to-back drama, and he wasn't beating the brakes off me, believe that. He slapped me three times and then there was the grand finale, but you'll hear more about that later. However, that was four encounters too many.

The real issue is that when you are with someone who is not satisfied with himself, or the relationship, there will be cheating and other issues. I truly believe that a satisfied and happy man won't cheat, and I have yet to find a scenario that has proven me wrong. In fact, a wise, old, man once said that he had never seen a full man eating off another plate. Guess what full also means? Satisfied! Unfortunately, guys typically aren't lining up to express their insecurities. They usually act out, and as women, the first thing that we think is, "There is something that I'm not doing right." This is where "Ride or Die" and "Down A**" chicks are made, in the mind of a broken woman who wants to satisfy her broken man.

Here is where I thank God for the women in my family because while their advice sometimes came from a toxic place, they always taught us to have boundaries. So, I refused to do anything sexually degrading—including a ménage a trois—make a drug sale, or rob or kill anyone, for example. I also didn't drink, and smoke weed, and I didn't care how anyone felt about it or who was partaking. Those were some of my boundaries. However, I've heard several stories about how a woman allowed another woman into her bed, delivered drugs or used drugs just to satisfy him. Most of them will tell you that the more they did to please him, the more he wanted. Why? Because in most cases, she wasn't the problem in the first place. You can give a man everything you've got, and if he doesn't want it from you, he'll treat your everything like nothing. Oftentimes, he's wounded, and he wants that everything from his mother, which is why I advise my clients to find out what kind of relationship he had with his "first love."

I loved his mother. She always kept it real with me when it came to advice. However, when there was a situation, I learned quickly that she would cover her son. It only took one "He ain't here" for me to understand the dynamics that I was dealing with. I was cool with it though because I knew what to expect. As a woman, she kicked it with me and put me up on game. However, she was still his mother, and I loved her as if she was mine. One day, she said something that stuck with me. "A man will only do what you let him do." I had never heard that because the women in my family were at the "I wish a n***a would" stage. I still didn't understand how I was "letting him" do anything because I thought I was punishing him by not speaking to him for days after he had stayed out all night and by staying at *work when I knew it irritated him. It's so funny to even write that now. There were clearly no consequences for his indiscretions. Therefore, they got worse!*

My overtime had stopped because the CEO was no longer at the agency. I knew that it would be temporary, but I STILL had the knowledge that I acquired. Nonetheless, I was home a lot more now, and I started to realize just how much we had grown apart. One day, he was warming up my car with the keys in the ignition as he ironed his pants. I was sleep when he burst through the door telling me to call the police and report my car stolen. Imagine being awakened to the shouts of your man, who hated the police, telling you to call them. My nerves were shot for days! We eventually found my car, but I didn't feel safe with it anymore because someone had the other set of keys. So, one day, I went to the dealership just to see what they had. Do I need to tell you what happened? Yep, I rolled out of there with a new car, but that wasn't my intent. When I rolled up with that car, the first words out of his mouth were, "Oh, m*thaf*kers going to get cars with woodgrain and sh*t." I quickly realized that *something had happened to us that I couldn't explain. Now I understand that our love had been trumped by competition, but I wasn't trying to outshine him. I thought we were on the same team. So, I laughed his comment off.*

The next couple of months were tough because we had grown apart so much. So, I thought I would cook his favorite meal to lighten the mood, and since it was a Friday night, I thought we would have some fun, if you know what I mean. I hopped on the freeway to go to the grocery store. I was almost at my exit when I heard a familiar ringtone. It was my best friend, and after hearing that my man was kicking it with my best friend's cousin, I got off the freeway and proceeded to go home. He wasn't getting dinner. As a matter of fact, I didn't care if he ever ate again.

When I pulled up, he was sitting in the car with his friend, mad about a separate incident, where once again, I didn't do anything inappropriate, but in his mind, I was guilty. He started with the usual ranting about how he was moving. He was packing his things and taking them outside to his car—all the while, he just kept talking. I was quiet until I couldn't take it anymore. So, I asked him was he going to ole girl's house and mentioned the name of my friend's cousin that I wasn't supposed to know about. He stopped dead in his tracks with his mouth wide open. Now it was my turn to go in, and I did. I was all the way turned up as the kids say. I talked myself so angry that I grabbed a boot that he had dropped and launched it at him. "You forgot your boot!" I screamed. It hit him in the face, and before I knew it, we were tussling.

We knocked the plexiglass window out on the porch. I faintly heard my grandmother, who lived next door, saying, "Y'all stop!" I was hurt, heartbroken, embarrassed, and just tired of him. He pulled his gun out to scare me and stop me from swinging, but I didn't care. I was tired of him, tired of the relationship, and I was working too hard to keep things together. I swung for every time I had saved money, and he went to jail, causing me to start over. I swung for every time I received a phone call from a chick. I swung for every sleepless night. I swung for every tear I cried. I swung for the baby he had on me. I swung for every disrespectful thing he had ever said to me. I swung for the three times he slapped me. I swung because he had the nerve to cheat where I grew up. I swung because I was just tired of him, and I didn't care what he did with that gun. I kept swinging.

They finally separated us, and this time, he was bleeding, not profusely, but enough to get his attention. I know he could have hurt me if he wanted to, but in a way, I think he knew that he deserved every hit, so he didn't fight back. He left, and I went to my bedroom and cried myself to sleep. That wasn't the last time he did something hurtful to me, but it was the last time I cried myself to sleep over him. I'm not sure if that is a good thing though because that means the dysfunction became normal.

Almost a year later, I started feeling uneasy about driving a newer-modeled car that was worth more than our house. I mean, I loved my hood—and still do. Shout out to Exit 44—but when the appraiser said how much the house was worth, I knew it was time to go. I was scared though. I had never lived on my own, and although I was still at the law firm, I wasn't sure if I could handle everything. My checks were as stacked as they had been when I was working sunup to sundown. Then he said it, "Maybe we should get our own place." I was ecstatic. Sure, he was gone half of the time, but maybe this would make him stay home! I mean, think about it, every man wants to be the king of his own castle, right? So, one day while I was riding in my childhood neighborhood—shout out to River Rouge—and saw a sign in the front yard of a beautiful set of apartments, I stopped and filled out an application. Then I got the call, and just like that, we had our own place.

Everything was coming together. I bought the dinette set and had bedroom furniture. My daughter loved sitting on the carpet together. She never even paid attention to the fact that we had no living room furniture. It didn't matter though. It was cozy, clean, and ours. I made sure the refrigerator, cabinets, and drinks were stocked. I didn't even drink, but just in case he had company, I had liquor and wine ready for them. Every morning, I cooked him a bacon, egg, and cheese sandwich to go, and on the weekends, I cooked waffles, pancakes, or whatever he had a taste for. I always cooked

*enough at dinner for him and the fellas to have
lunch the next day too. I even prepared a Super
Bowl feast, and he didn't even watch football. I just
wanted him home, so I did everything—within my
boundaries—to keep him satisfied. Then it
happened.*

*It was about 12:30 a.m. I was finishing the kitchen
after a late dinner. Everyone was sleep, and finally,
after a day of work and school, I could get some
shuteye. Just as I climbed in the bed, the house
telephone rang. It was her, you remember, the one
who had delivered three weeks before me. Four
years had passed, and I just wished she would go
away! She probably felt the same thing about me. I
nudged him so hard and put the phone to his ear.
He sat straight up in the bed like he had a
nightmare. Then he hung the telephone up. I pointed
at the door. He asked why he had to leave.
Meanwhile, the telephone was ringing back-to-
back. He unplugged the phone. I just pointed at the
door. He kept talking about how he could just sleep
in the living room like his friends did when they
messed up. I just pointed at the door because there
was no way that he was going to sleep anywhere*

near me that night! He kept pleading because he didn't want me to answer that phone, and he knew when he left, I would answer it. He finally left, and as soon as I plugged the telephone up, it was STILL ringing. I answered the telephone and told her that he was on his way to her house. She said that their baby needed some diapers. Now, my daughter was four years old. She had her daughter three weeks before my daughter. So, her words could only mean one thing... they had another baby.

My heart sank. I hung up the telephone. After about an hour, she called back. He never made it there. I told her that I didn't know where he was, but she should take care of her child. She didn't call back. I thought he had finally made it to her house, but the whole time, he was at my mother's house. Once again, I had gone to great lengths to give him what he said he wanted, and he still wasn't satisfied. Now that I'm wiser, I realize he wasn't satisfied with himself, and therefore, nothing that I provided was enough. You will NEVER be right for the wrong person. However, the hardest thing in relationships is knowing whether we should stay and wait for them to change, or walk away?

RELEASING/REPAIRING TOXIC RELATIONSHIPS

"Letting go means coming to the realization that some people are a part of your history, not a part of your destiny." ~ Steve Maraboli

"God is able to fix that which is broken so that what stands repaired is immeasurably greater than that which stood before it needed repair. Therefore, the most staggering brokenness conceivable is in reality the greatest opportunity imaginable." ~ Craig D. Lounsbrough

CHAPTER 6: STAY OR WALK AWAY?

As a relationship coach, clients come to me for an answer to the question, "Do I stay or walk away?" However, they usually know the answer in their hearts before the question leaves their lips. Yet, there are times when God requires us to release people we want to keep and keep people we want to release. Here's where my expertise kicks in because I understand how many, and even you, may have this dilemma. Do I release or repair? Do I stay or walk away? These are tough questions. Where do we start? I'm a teacher, so let's start at the root of what these words, release or repair, really mean regarding relationships.

Repairing means to fix or restore back to an operative state. Sometimes it means restoring the item back to an even better state than it was previously. Think about a car. When you have car trouble, you take your car to the repair shop or to someone who can repair it. When you pick up the car, sometimes it's not only operating better than it was before, but it may drive better than it did when you purchased it. Well, it's the same for those who have heartache. Depending on the level of toxicity, they come to the shop—a counselor, a life coach, a social worker, etc.—to repair their relationships, but their bleeding hearts must first be fixed at the root.

Most of us know what releasing means, but when it comes to relationships, the lines are blurred. How do you completely release someone that you have children with? How do you completely release someone when you have built relationships with their families and vice versa? How do you completely release someone when you can't stop thinking about him? How do you completely release someone when you can't stop thinking about what could have been done differently so you can grow old together like he promised?

See, releasing means to let go, but when it comes to relationships, what do we do with the memories, children and other things that don't walk out of the door with him? What happens when he makes a fuss about the new man around his children? What happens when he uses the children to see you? Don't get me wrong, there are solutions to all these questions, but it takes…TIME! So, if you loved someone and/or shared a portion of your life with him, release becomes a process, instead of a one-time ordeal.

Most clients want a quick fix for the relationship because they want to remain with their mate, but they want him to change. Again, a man will change when he sees the gain in keeping you or is afraid to lose you. Otherwise, he won't change, especially if you have allowed his ill behavior without consequence. Sure, you put him out for a few days, blocked his calls, and/or changed your number, but if none of this is followed by a firm decision to move on with actions to match, you are simply wasting your time.

See, you must rely on what you believe. Why? Because God knows the heart and future of man. This means He may tell you to stay because He knows your mate will change. He may also tell you to go before you waste years of your life because He knows your mate won't change. Hence, we must remain connected to our GPS (God's Protective System), and trust Him, no matter how bad it hurts or how frustrating it gets because He knows the future. I will, however, go out on a limb and say that God won't instruct us to repair a toxic situation where there is no love at the foundation. Why? God is LOVE, and love (GOD) is the only thing stronger than trust. In fact, love (GOD) is the only thing that can hold a relationship together until trust is re-established. So, if you are questioning whether you should release or repair a toxic relationship, ask yourself the following questions:

1) Are you willing to change? You are the only one you control, and no matter what, you aren't blameless. If nothing else, you have allowed this destructive behavior to continue without consequence. There are always red flags.

2) Does he see anything wrong with his actions? If so, is he willing to change? Sometimes we are waiting for someone to change who is either content or doesn't see anything wrong with his actions. You can fight with him, but you should never fight him for change.

3) Has the pain of remaining the same exceeded the pain of change? This is when you know you can't continue in this way. It's like you wake up one day and think, "This is not it, and something has got to give." Pain is often a catalyst for change, but it's up to you how much you will endure. When it came to my situation, my grandmother always said, "She'll be done when she gets tired." She was right!

4) Where is love in this? This is a hard question for many to answer because lust, pity and obligation are also mistaken for love. However, if you ask, where is GOD in this, the question is much easier to answer. Love conquers all, and with God, all things are possible. Yet, repairing with and in love, doesn't always mean that you continue to reside with the person or that the relationship is restored to what it was before. It simply means that God can mend the brokenness of the relationship, and when brokenness is removed, toxicity can't thrive. So, we begin to heal and forgive. God will then lead us in the safest way to move forward concerning them, and sometimes, that's

from a distance. Whatever the case, you can't repair effectively, without love in your foundation.

Neither releasing or repairing presents a quick fix. Most of us want to release a person because in the heat of distress, it is the quickest and easiest option. However, if we are honest, the residue of our broken hearts last long after that relationship door shuts. Remember those memories, families and situations I presented a few pages back? Yes, he may be gone physically, but it can take years for you to totally move on because you aren't honest with yourself about the hurt and rejection that remains in your heart. When we don't take time to heal, we will bleed on those who didn't cut us. But society says that something must be wrong with us if we are alone and we buy into that perspective, moving swiftly into relationship after relationship. Over time, we become numb to the pain that we are carrying, so much that it no longer feels heavy to you. The truth is, you have no idea how heavy the hurt is until it's lifted.

If you take nothing else from this chapter, please know that there are no quick fixes when it comes to digging up root issues, and therefore, many just don't endure the process. Whether you choose to release or repair, know that you have what it takes to get through it. I know because I was at the point of decision, and because the pain of remaining the same presented more agony than the pain of change, I knew it was time to release. God (LOVE) wasn't in the midst. My heart couldn't take anymore, and my mind had already tapped out.

I couldn't believe what I heard. Another baby? Why was he doing this to me? I was working hard, going to school, and building our dream. Everything I was doing, I did for us. Then I started to think about it. The more I accomplished, the more he resented me. I never threw it up in his face. I supported him through the good and the bad. When I shopped for my daughter, I shopped for his because I considered her to be mine when I forgave him. I treated his family as my own. I just didn't understand why he was treating me this way. The fatigue of a wondering mind, a wounded heart, and teary eyes final caught up with me, and I fell asleep.

The next day, I went to work, and when I came to pick up our daughter at the sitter's house, he was there. I had managed to avoid him all day, but he knew he would catch me there. He told me that she was lying and just trying to break us up because he didn't want her anymore. When I asked him point blank if they had another child together, he looked me in the eyes and said, "No!" My heart was so happy, but my mind was screaming, "GIRLLLLL, don't believe that!" The problem is that it wasn't hard to believe that she would lie because she had lied so many times, but then again, so had he. However, I chose to believe my man. So, he was back home like nothing ever happened.

This time, he was doing right. He came home every night at a reasonable time. He was even paying his part of the bills consistently. We were getting along so well that he started talking about marriage. Then one day, there was a terrible snowstorm. Our offices were closed, so I was home for the day. I fixed breakfast, and he decided that he was going to stay in for the day after meeting two people who owed him money. He left out, and I laid down. I had been tired the last couple of weeks, so the day off came right on time.

The electricity had gone out because of the storm, so I was laying in silence, until my cellular phone rang. It was him, but his voice was different. Something was wrong. I sat up in the bed when I heard him say, "Baby, please don't leave me.

Please promise you ain't gone leave me." I was startled because I was just dozing off, so I asked, "Why would I leave you? What's going on?" The words after that destroyed me emotionally. He told me he had an argument with HER, and she ran in the house and left his kids in the car, so he took them. When I heard kids, I was devastated, not because of what he had done, but because I knew he lied when he said there wasn't another baby, but my deceitful heart took over and believed what my mind knew was a lie.

I checked back into the conversation as he said he needed to call me back because someone was blowing up his cell phone. I was thinking, Fool, you just took that woman's children, of course your phone is blowing up! Then he called back, and with all the audacity in the world, told me that the police said that if he brought the kids back, there would be no charges or arrests. So, he asked me to take them back for him and said that he would have someone ride with me to make sure I was safe. I was still trying to wrap my head around how a quiet, cozy day in the house, with breakfast, lunch, and dinner, turned into a nightmare? I opened my mouth to say no, but yes came out. Here I was, devastated, and still protecting him. I picked the children up, and he looked at me as if he knew our relationship would never be the same.

I drove across town, and as I turned onto the block, police were everywhere. They instructed me to pull over, and they took the guy who rode with me, to the back of a police car. The female officer began to interrogate me about my mate's whereabouts. They made me pop my trunk, and she threatened to take me to jail. When the lady officer walked away to converse with her partners, I called my mother and told her they were going to take me to jail. I told her where my bail money was and to let him know that if I set foot in that jail, we were done forever.

Eleven minutes later (it was a 30-minute drive on a regular day), I saw him walking up the street with his hands up in a soaked hoodie. They put him in the squad car facing me, and he kept mouthing that he loved me as he looked through the seats of the police car. They finally let the guy who rode with me out of the squad car, and when he got in the car, he told me that SHE had lied and told the police that my mate had shot up the house because she heard him say that his fiancée was bringing the kids back. Guess who bailed him out and went to court with him?

After he got out and came home, things went back to normal. We never had a conversation about the new addition or anything. He went back to being on his best behavior, so I didn't bring it up either. I really wished it wasn't true, so I acted as if it wasn't. Two weeks later, at 4 a.m., I was in the bathroom regurgitating and peeing at the same time. This happened about a week straight before I realized it wasn't food poisoning and my cycle had not come. Surely, it was stress that had pushed it off schedule. I prayed that it was stress because I couldn't imagine having baby number four with someone who had not acknowledged baby number three.

CONCLUSION

"Tell your story. Express your truth. How people respond to it says more about them than you. Those who judge will one day eat the fruit of their own lips. Be free!" ~ Zakiya Monique

CHAPTER 7: THE NUMBER OF COMPLETION

After all that, you are probably asking why I stayed? I stayed for the same reason most women do. I thought he would change. I thought the other woman would win. I thought he would realize how good of a woman I was. I thought I could do something differently to make him happy, including minimize my accomplishments. Now I understand that I wasn't too much, at the time, but he just didn't want much. He later admitted that himself.

One thing I stand firmly on as a relationship coach over twenty-two years later is that it doesn't matter what I tell my clients or how any examples I give, until they reach the breaking point, until they have had enough, they will stay. Just as I did. Nevertheless, my experience doesn't allow me to judge, for I have experienced enough to be judged. I try to think of what I needed at that time. It was love, prayer, and wisdom, not judgment.

> *It was summertime, and we were on and off, as usual. This time felt a little different though. Our physical encounters had changed. He no longer handled me as gently as he used to. I started back working long hours to avoid the whole situation.*

Three days straight, I had dreams that I couldn't understand. I went to church, and the sermon was about completion and how seven is the number of completion. We had just celebrated seven years together, but the truth is, I was with him for seven years. He was wounded, and true love was so foreign to him that he rejected the unfamiliar. I began to question if he loved me, because I didn't believe that he loved himself.

He called me after church. He jokingly told me that he was going to buy me a gun earlier that day, but he decided against it because he thought I would use it on him. My response was, "You're probably right because I've been having these dreams." When I told him about the dreams, he was speechless to the point where he told me he had to call me back.

Later that evening, when he thought I was in for the night, I bumped into him and a new chick at the gas station. Instantly, I realized what each of the dreams meant. The first dream told me her first name. The second dream told me her last name. The third dream told me they had been staying at a motel because I dreamed that he was sitting on the side of a freshly made bed with numbers on the outside door. I realized, in that moment, why he was speechless when I explained the dreams.

The funny thing is, she wasn't new to me because I knew her from my neighborhood. Isn't that something? Everyone knew about them, even my family, but no one said a thing for several reasons, some reasons that I now understand and others that I will probably never understand. Meanwhile, he pulled off, and I went in the gas station and bought my items.

I never cried about it. I tried so hard to let it out. There wasn't anything to let out. I was all out of tears and all out of fears. I knew it could never go back to what it was. I would never see him in the same way. I beat myself up for a long time, thinking that I should've worked less and given him more attention. However, I don't think the relationship would have lasted. We grew apart. I was after something that I always knew I was made for, and he didn't believe he was made for more than what he was doing at that time. We continued to see each

other on and off for a while, then we tried the
friendship thing, and after too much drama, we
realized that it was best to just move on.

I often wonder if I would have ever had the strength to leave him if circumstances were different. Though I wouldn't have wanted to leave, I knew we were growing in two different directions, and I wasn't willing to abandon my goals and dreams for anyone. After all, my daughter needed me to be a better example than I had seen. My purpose needed to be fulfilled. I had not worked this hard to minimize my accomplishments for someone that I thought was a teammate but was a loving opponent. Don't get me wrong, I don't believe his heart was against me. However, there was a war going on within him concerning how he perceived my progress, and in my mind, either you are with me 100% or not. There is no in between.

Yes, my loyalty was often interpreted to others as stupidity, and in no way am I advocating for this. I was talked about and judged by many, maybe even you as you read this book. People often said that I was too smart to go through this, but trust me, the enemy will use anyone or anything to derail your progress and delay or even deny your purpose. But what the enemy meant for evil, God made it all good. You never know how you will gain the experience necessary to fuel your purpose. So, I don't regret going through the things I've experienced because my story has touched the lives of many around the world. I pray it has in some way touched you too. There is truly no failure if you learn and make your pain pay you. Therefore, every time I empower youth, recovering addicts, and other women, or serve as a much-needed outlet for wounded men, I'm indeed, satisfied.

Every ending makes room for a beginning!

The Author

Born in an era where going outside and watching television was the thing to do, Zakiya Monique stayed in, read books, and loved to write. In fact, watching television was used as punishment for her. She loved to tell stories and quickly became known for her attention to detail as she eloquently painted pictures in the minds of those who listened.

In 2008, at one of her lowest points, there was a prophetic word given that she would write books. She chuckled because she had gotten away from her love for writing. Then in 2014, she was given the task by her pastor to write a movie. Again, she had not written anything in years, but desired to be obedient. The finished product reduced her to tears, not just because of the faithfulness of God, but because she was reunited with her love for writing and storytelling.

In 2016, her purpose, speaking and coaching, was revealed, and Zakiya Monique and Company, LLC was established. Two years later, Zakiya realized writing could also assist her clients in their healing processes as it had done for her throughout the years. Yet she couldn't imagine someone refusing her clients or changing how her clients should tell their stories, so she established Dauntless Knight Publishing, LLC in 2018.

Thank You

Thank you for reading my book! I pray the information was what you needed to move to the next level in your relationships.

As you know, many people purchase items based on reviews. So, if you enjoyed this read, please take a moment to provide me with a review. Go to my Amazon Author Page (https://www.amazon.com/author/zakiyamonique), click on the book and leave your review.

While you're online leaving the review, let's connect! I can't wait to hear from you on my social media live videos. Click on the links below and join me today.

Facebook: www.facebook.com/ladyz.monique
Instagram: www.instagram.com/zakiyamoniquespeaks

For coaching or speaking engagements, contact me via email at zakiyamoniqueandco@gmail.com.

Again, thank you for your support, and watch out for those...
Killer Connections!

www.ingramcontent.com/pod-product-compliance
Lightning Source LLC
Chambersburg PA
CBHW071230290326
41931CB00037B/2571